THE CLASSIC ENGLISH
GARDENING GUIDES

PLANTING IN
PATTERNS

THE CLASSIC ENGLISH
GARDENING GUIDES

PLANTING IN PATTERNS

PATRICK TAYLOR

SERIES EDITOR
PENELOPE HOBHOUSE

1817

HARPER & ROW, PUBLISHERS, New York
Cambridge, Philadelphia, San Francisco, London
Mexico City, São Paulo, Singapore, Sydney

First Published in Great Britain in 1989 by
PAVILION BOOKS LIMITED

The Classic English Gardening Guides
PLANTING IN PATTERNS

Copyright © 1989 by Patrick Taylor

Designed by Bridgewater Design

First US edition.

Library of Congress Cataloging-in-Publication Data available upon request.

ISBN 0-06-016124-8

LC 89-45045

Printed and bound in West Germany

89   90   91   92   93   10   9   8   7   6   5   4   3   2   1

PUBLISHER'S NOTE

Unlike botanical names, the common names for plants are
governed by no international rules. For this gardening
series we have adopted The National Trust style which is
to use initial capitals for common names referring to a single
species. Where the name consists of two or more words, the
first letter of each word is capitalised. General names which
refer to a number of species are not capitalised. All common
names are printed in roman.

C O N T E N T S

THE PATTERNED PLOT

What is a garden? Most of us would answer – a place where we grow plants. Historically it is a place of seclusion and enclosure, giving protection from the predatory world outside. 'Garden' is linguistically connected with the words 'guard' and 'haven' (indeed the Danish for a garden is *have*). 'Garden' also suggests a perfect and ordered world – distinct from the disordered world of nature. And in this privileged environment it was possible to grow ornamental plants – protected from the elements and from marauding animals. In ancient Persia where the climate made horticultural survival an even chancier matter, they called a garden *pairidaeza*, an enclosure, but which came to mean an earthly heaven.

This essential garden idea – a perfect patch in an imperfect world – still lurks insistently behind the earthy matter of horticulture. It is partly a matter of a privileged environment in which plants can flourish more vigorously than in nature and partly the idea of an ordered world that can be arranged harmoniously. This book is concerned with ways of ordering a garden using growing structural elements; it is about the patterns of planting that give shape and coherence. These patterns are made of hedges, rhythmic repetitions, the structural arrangement of plants on arbours or pergolas, the architecture of topiary or the patchwork of parterres. In Britain our ideal garden is, perhaps, one in which nature is happily accommodated in a formal setting. By 'formal' I do not mean the nature-

Pattern and structure of box-hedges and yew topiary harmoniously intertwined in the intricate parterres of the Great Garden at Pitmedden.

crushing megalomania of André Le Nôtre – I mean a disciplined framework, an orderly setting from which the wildness of nature is not necessarily entirely excluded.

In Europe there are perhaps only two kinds of garden. One might be called the garden of display – of which Le Nôtre's or 'Capability' Brown's giant landscapes are the great examples. The other might be called the garden of privacy which aims to provide a peaceful setting in which conversations may take place, things be admired, spirits recharged – the agreeable life of the sitting room extended out of doors. Of the second kind are the courtyard gardens of Islam, the enclosed medieval garden or the intricate compartmentalized garden of the Italian Renaissance.

In Britain, despite the immense upheavals of the eighteenth-century landscape revolution followed by the restlessly eclectic nineteenth century, it is to this second, enclosed type of garden that we tend to return. And by its nature the enclosed garden tends towards formality. There have been, from time to time, great battles between proponents of formal and informal, or 'natural', gardening. By the last quarter of the nineteenth century William Robinson, with his theories of 'natural' gardening, was seen as the great scourge of formality. In 1892 Reginald Blomfield published his formidable counterblast to Robinson, *The Formal Garden in England*. Here he effectively mocks the ideas of the 'natural' gardeners – 'anyone who wants natural scenery will want the real thing; he will hardly be content to sit in his rockery and suppose himself to be among the mountains.' Blomfield regretted the loss of all the great formal gardens that existed in the early eighteenth century which were swept away in the

In the Long Garden at Cliveden the lively pattern of hedges, topiary and geometric shapes in box and yew gives firm structure.

craze for landscape gardening. Above all he stressed the importance of a firm visual relationship between house and garden. In fact there was plenty of common ground in Robinson's and Blomfield's positions. There was much formality in Robinson's own garden at Gravetye Manor with its straight paths, wisteria pergolas and ivy-covered bowers. The great twentieth-century gardener Russell Page sums it up in his book *The Education of a Gardener*: 'The discussion between the adherents of "formal" and "informal" gardening still continues, offering little but a display of partial understanding on both sides. For the "informalists" I would rather say that a garden which is after all a humanisation of nature and intended to be for "convenience and delight" needs, like all man-made structures, a framework. Its different parts need connecting in some kind of order . . . whether this order, this sequence of spaces be formal in its detail or not is really of secondary importance.'

Since the Second World War informality has been a powerful influence on garden style in Britain. 'Cottage gardening', in one form or another, has been the overwhelming influence. Vita Sackville-West described that lordly garden HIDCOTE as 'a cottage garden on the most glorified scale.' In the hands of gardeners less skilled than Lawrence Johnston, the maker of Hidcote, this tradition makes a virtue of the unkempt look and regards weeds as the welcome presence of nature in one's own patch.

In Britain we have a passion for plants. The benign climate has allowed the introduction of an immense range of exotic garden plants from many parts of the world, and we have become obsessed with them. This obsession frequently results in the garden becoming a collection of plants in which the individual merits of the plant and, to a certain degree, colour harmony, are seen as the essence. The structure of the garden and the pattern of the different parts becomes correspondingly neglected.

Gardens are, of course, about plants but they are also, first and foremost, about composition. In our passion for plantsmanship we tend to neglect design. 'If the main lines of a composition are right,' Russell Page wrote, 'the detail may be left to take care of itself.' Time spent planning a garden – rather than in an uncontrolled frenzy of plant buying – is of the essence.

At Canons Ashby the monumental shapes of old yew topiary repeat the vertical emphasis of the statue and gate-piers.

Where gravel paths intersect in the rose garden at Mottisfont Abbey the solid presence of Irish yews soaring above the borders adds permanent structure to the ephemeral herbaceous planting.

Two of the key elements in the patterns of garden design are structural and ornamental planting. By structural planting I mean permanent planting whose chief purpose is to define the spaces of a garden. By ornamental planting I mean permanent incidental planting whose primary purpose is decorative. In the finest gardens the two, of course, go hand in hand. An impeccably kept hedge of yew, with its rich dark green foliage, may be both a key structural element and decorative in its own right. Equally, ornament may provide the structure. In the

In the Pool Garden at Crathes Castle the richly planted herbaceous borders derive pattern and structure from the repeated plantings of the copper-leaved Cotinus coggygria *'Foliis Purpureis'. In winter the structure is austerely attractive.*

great topiary garden at LEVENS HALL (Cumbria) structure and ornament work together in the profusion of clipped shapes.

To many gardeners and garden visitors the most satisfying gardens of all are made *only* from design ingredients, both 'soft' and 'hard' – hedges, topiary, paths and walls. They do not depend for their successes in any way at all on exotic plants or elaborate border schemes. In addition, a really strong and carefully worked out scheme of structural planting is one that will enhance all kinds of subsequent planting of flowering shrubs, herbaceous perennials and other primarily ornamental plants.

The planting, for example, of a great Italian garden may consist only of bay, box, ilex, cypress and yew. This extremely limited range of plants is none the less capable of enormous spatial variety. And those gardens that do use a very wide range of plants succeed only if the garden has been laid out with a very firm structure (for example CRATHES and HIDCOTE). All gardeners are liable to be seduced by some beautiful, rare and irresistible plant. It is the mark of the successful gardener to be able to accommodate impulse acquisitions of this kind because the structure of the garden is strong enough to hold them. Margery Fish, writing about TINTINHULL, praised the harmony of different flowers and shapes: 'This is achieved by choosing plants that fit in with a preconceived plan and not because of their individual attraction. This does not mean there are not unusual plants in the garden. There are many, but they have been chosen so cleverly that one sees the garden as a whole first and discovers the many treasures in it afterwards.'

Most structural planting is made of evergreen plants – though a few deciduous plants have their special virtues too. Thus it is permanent from season to season although most evergreens do vary subtly in their seasonal colouring and the appearance of the structural planting will, of course, be greatly affected by other planting. The silhouette, for example, of a box-edged border may seem sharp

A clairvoyée cut into a yew hedge at Sissinghurst makes a decorative visual link between the South Cottage garden and the rose garden.

and linear in winter or early spring. These lines may be strikingly softened in the spring by, say, a planting of tulips and, in high summer, by billowing drifts of herbaceous plants. Equally, a yew hedge as the backdrop to a primarily herbaceous border will, in winter, assume a much more severe appearance. The interaction between structural planting and ephemeral decorative planting may be a source of satisfying variety in a garden, altering the mood decisively with the passage of the seasons. At SISSINGHURST the north end of the celebrated white garden is, in fact, a formal parterre of box hedges and cubes arranged geometrically. This pattern is firmly predominant until high summer when it is all but lost in an explosion of white and silver.

Structural planting defines the very boundaries of the garden itself and its different internal parts. It may do this in the form of a barrier like the hedges (the subject of Chapter 2), which can be sufficiently high to obscure one part of the garden from another or low enough to outline different compartments, borders, paths or other garden features. It may also afford a partially obscured view, as in an alley of pleached trees (see Chapter 3) that allow one to see below the level of the branches. This can have the effect of revealing an enticing glimpse beneath the foliage of some other part of the garden – encouraging further exploration. A similar, and extremely effective device is the opening (or *clairvoyée*), cut into a hedge or wall through which may be seen a view of the countryside beyond or of some other part of the garden. At BATEMAN'S, windows are cut into the boundary yew hedge showing views of pasture and woodland. At SISSINGHURST there is a round window in a yew hedge that separates the rose garden from the cottage garden. Some gardens seem quite isolated from their surroundings. Others capitalize on carefully focused views and refreshing glimpses of contrasting rural landscape. A spectacular example of this is the great double hedge of hornbeam that lines a wide grassy walk at HIDCOTE, at the end of which a pair of huge

Three-hundred-year-old beech hedges form dramatic green corridors at Levens Hall. They are now so wide that one can walk within them.

A passage of yew hedges at Sissinghurst provides a calm interval between different garden areas. The glimpsed opening encourages exploration.

wrought-iron gates frames a view of the Cotswold countryside. This is an effect which can be achieved in even quite small gardens. It is well worth while when planning a garden to think carefully of some feature (a church spire, an interesting building, or an attractive view) which may be framed, or to which the eye may be drawn, by some carefully designed structural arrangement. There may, equally, be something ugly which should be concealed or from which the eye should be distracted. It is always important to consider everything that is visible from one's garden. The surrounding tree-line, and the way in which its silhouette strikingly frames the sky, is an extremely important part of a garden's visual boundary.

Another valuable use of hedges is to provide a contrasting or linking passage in the garden. One may want a cool green corridor between two thematically different parts of the garden – for example to give a feeling of repose after the busy-ness of an overflowing summer border. The Yew Walk at SISSINGHURST is a good example of this. It separates an intensively cultivated and formal part of the garden, the Tower Lawn and the White Garden, from the informality of the orchard with its long grass, naturalized bulbs and sprawling fruit trees. Structural plantings can also mediate between very different ingredients. In front of the cool, gentlemanly, Georgian façade of HINTON AMPNER is a surprisingly informal cherry orchard – but it is bordered by neatly clipped box hedges and punctuated by smooth cones of yew. These architectural elements provide a visual link between the urbane house and the rural orchard.

Hedges and walls are the most satisfactory divisions for gardens (such as HIDCOTE and SISSINGHURST) that are divided into compartments with very different themes and effects. The same kind of hedging material used repeatedly in a garden has a powerful unifying effect, however great the variety of planting schemes. Hedges, like paths, can also direct the eye and suggest a route. It can be distressingly unrestful to find oneself in one part of a garden and have no clear idea about where to go to next.

The size and positioning of hedges can be manipulated to create optical illusions and make gardens seem much bigger (or, of course, smaller) than they are. Twin hedges that converge slightly as they recede, emphasizing linear perspective, will make a distance seem much greater. This illusion can be made even more powerful if the height of the hedges progressively decreases. In a small garden this can be extremely effective, but one should guard against making the effect too emphatic – the effect of illusion is quickly lost if it seems contrived or exaggerated. There is a tendency at the end of any vista of this sort to place some kind of eye-catcher – an urn, bench or whatever. The absence of such a punctuation mark can, in fact, arouse pleasurable feelings of anticipation – one feels there *must* be something to be explored. The expressive use of structural planting in this way – and a very restrained use of ornaments – is one of the most satisfying of all garden design skills. Less may indeed be more. Russell Page said 'I could consider no modern garden even remotely interesting as a work of art unless it could stand as such, stripped of every single purely decorative attribute. A garden artist will only use decoration to heighten the style, that is, the idea from which his whole construction has sprung.' The extent to which expectations are fulfilled or denied – the mixture of familiar themes and dramatic surprises – is an important element in garden design.

The avenue (dealt with in more detail in Chapter 3) is another important form of patterned planting that gives structure. By this I do not necessarily mean a couple of miles of ancient trees marching to the front door of a grand country house. The word avenue means 'a way of approach – a passage or path of entrance or exit'. In gardening terms this can mean parallel rows of regularly placed objects (not necessarily plants) spaced out to line a path or view. At TINTINHULL an avenue of catmint is most effectively and appropriately used to compose the main

Hedges of box and cones of yew give structure to the informal cherry orchard at Hinton Ampner linking it visually to the house.

axis of the ornamental kitchen garden. The traditional avenue has practical as well as structural value; it provides an excellent windbreak and is, for this reason, especially common in open, windswept places such as at WIMPOLE HALL in Cambridgeshire. In structural terms the avenue can serve several different purposes. It can draw the eye away towards some other point, as it does at ERDDIG where an avenue of Portugal Laurel (*Prunus lusitanica*) links house and canal. It can emphasize some view or object – in particular the façade of a house. The avenue of Common Limes (*Tilia × europaea*) that lines the north drive at CLIVEDEN is the same width as the house. The

scale is important. In an open landscape there is no limit to the size of tree – they can be as big as the biggest tree will grow. An avenue of such trees that seem to march out of view over the horizon is a spectacular sight. In the twentieth century few avenues on that scale have been planted. At ANGLESEY ABBEY a remarkable quadruple avenue of alternating Horse Chestnuts (*Aesculus hippocastanum*) and London Planes (*Platanus × acerifolia*) was planted in the 1930s. Within the confines of a garden, an avenue can have a presence so powerful as to overwhelm less emphatic features. It must be carefully judged to fit harmoniously with the other ingredients. At WIGHTWICK

At Pitmedden a central avenue of yew obelisks set in a broad walk of turf forms a strong axis connecting the entrance stairs with the gate on the opposite side. It also provides breathing space between the busy parterres that flank it.

MANOR an avenue of yew drums on the south terrace marches away from the house. They are 3m/10ft in diameter, and as much high, and have grown so close that one can only just pass between. They have a rather sinister presence – like the left-over temple of some forgotten religion.

The effect of repeated planting is often both structural and ornamental. The unconstrained planting of a mixed border, for example, may be given a firm pattern by the repetition of some structural shape. For example, rows of yews – or some other strongly architectural plant – progressing regularly down a border, can provide a strong architectural presence to pin down more exuberant, informal planting below. At HIDCOTE clipped pillars of Common Yew (*Taxus baccata*) have a calming effect on borders of billowing peonies. An avenue of unclipped Irish Yews (*Taxus baccata* 'Fastigiata') at HINTON AMPNER makes an excellent formal counterpoint to the banks of sprawling shrub roses on either side. There are all kinds of plants that can be used in such a unifying way. At SISSINGHURST Vita Sackville-West made rhythmic plantings of the small pink-flowered rowan *Sorbus cashmiriana* in beds of old roses (west of the 'Rondel'). Their neat shapes rise regularly above the mass of roses below. In addition, their beautiful flowers in the spring and striking autumn colour and glistening white berries in winter provide interest when the roses are not performing. Planting of this kind need not be formal. At BUSCOT PARK Peter Coats designed a pair of symmetrical borders in yellow and blue which face each other across a path. These borders are primarily herbaceous but rows of the ornamental golden-leaved acacia (*Robinia pseudoacacia* 'Frisia') give permanent structure. I find this tree difficult to site; its intense leaf colour can seem strident. Here it is soothed down by the presence of other yellows.

Fastigiate (i.e. tall, upright) trees are a valuable part of the vocabulary of patterned planting. Many are evergreen (yew, juniper, cypress) though there are fastigiate

An avenue of Irish yews at Hinton Ampner makes a formal contrast to the unconstrained bushes of old roses on either side.

Across the **parterre de broderie** *at Ashdown House the view is framed by a pair of billowing Irish yews. The formality of the house and the symmetrical garden, devoid of the colour of flowers, contrasts with the shaggy, unclipped yews.*

The shady tunnel at Ham House, with hedges of yew and canopy of hornbeam, has windows that give framed views of the knot garden beyond.

forms of several broad-leaved deciduous trees. These last must be treated carefully. In some, their oddness may be so overpowering as to upset a garden scheme. Undoubtedly, evergreen trees are more versatile and effective. A pair of Irish Yews makes an impressive entrance, or the grand frame for some spectacular view – as they do on either side of the parterres at ASHDOWN HOUSE. Irish Yews, if allowed to grow unrestricted, in time form handsome billowing shapes like misshapen goblets. Alternatively they may be clipped every year to make a great geometric outline. In a border or parterre tall geometric shapes can provide a telling contrast – bringing vertical features to the predominantly horizontal design. In the 'Italian' parterres at TATTON PARK Irish Junipers (*Juniperus communis* 'Hibernica') are used in this way.

The alley is, in effect, a kind of avenue on a more intimate scale. It should not be confused with the French *allée* which is a broad path, or ride, cut through woodland. Strictly speaking an alley is a pathway lined with high enclosing hedges. Today it is often made of pleached trees with the lower trunks kept bare of branches so that one may see below the foliage. Hornbeam and lime are the most frequently used trees but others with sufficiently pliant young branches are suitable.

Pergolas and tunnels (which I describe in more detail in Chapter 3) have similar functions. They form strong linear emphases and they provide an effective linking, or transitional, passage. They also provide shade and seclusion. The framework of a pergola generally remains visible and is in itself ornamental. It is used as a support for climbing and twining plants, usually not too densely planted so that other parts of the garden are visible and contrasting planting may be arranged at ground level. Almost any climbing plant may be used with a pergola. One sees foliage and flowers in a new way with the light shining through them. Plants with heavily scented flowers are especially effective – forming a deliciously perfumed shady path.

A tunnel resembles a pergola but the planting forms a dense mass that generally obscures, and may eventually supersede, the supporting framework so that it appears to be made only of living plants. For this purpose it is usual to choose plants that will in time form a substantial framework of their own. Ornamental trees are often chosen, especially those with pliable young growth that lends itself to pleaching. The famous laburnum tunnel at BODNANT is a striking example. Here the long golden racemes of *Laburnum* × *watereri* 'Vossii' hang down within the tunnel and seem to fill it with light. Tunnels of mixed fruit trees – say apples and pears – are extremely beautiful when in flower and in fruit. At PITMEDDEN a tunnel of apples is made of seventeenth-century varieties to fit the period of the garden.

Topiary – plants clipped and trained into ornamental shapes – can be at once decorative and structural, as Chapter 4 demonstrates. The traditional, and usually the most satisfactory, plants are yew or box. For more complicated shapes yew is to be preferred. It is completely hardy, takes very firm clipping well and puts out energetic new growth which may be tied and shaped. Box is less vigorous and is really at its best for very simple topiary – geometric shapes like cones, obelisks or pyramids. Topiary used with discretion can be a lively, and versatile, ingredient in a garden's structure. It can have great monumental presence (the 'grand pianos' made of yew at BLICKLING HALL are a good example) or it can soar ornamentally above other plantings. Topiary can be used to echo architectural forms. At the late-thirteenth-century CHIRK CASTLE old yew hedges clipped into giant castellated shapes, softened with age, make a harmonious green bastion to the house. In a setting of richly planted borders topiary can add a refreshingly sober note of contrast. A 200-year-old clipped Portugal Laurel (*Prunus lusitanica*) is

the focal point of radiating double herbaceous borders at CRATHES CASTLE – an emphatic glistening dome in a profusion of colour. Topiary can also be used to introduce a note of humour or whimsy, such as the hounds chasing a fox along a yew hedge at KNIGHTSHAYES COURT.

The features that are described in Chapter 5 – knots, mazes and parterres – are by definition patterns in themselves. Knots are best thought of as ornaments in the larger setting of some other piece of formal planting or as self-contained miniature gardens. They can look especially attractive filling a small courtyard and seen from the windows above. They need impeccable maintenance – an unkempt knot is indeed a depressing sight. Clippings must be carefully gathered and any gravel kept neatly raked and entirely free of weeds.

The maze, or labyrinth, is of great antiquity. As a

Old castellated yew hedges at Chirk Castle have lost their crisp outlines after years of clipping. They make a dramatic boundary separating the castle from the flower garden beyond and echoing the castle architecture in monumental plant shapes.

At Blickling Hall the garden on the east side has square herbaceous borders of harmonised colour schemes pinned down with rounded cones of yew at each corner. Further away massive 'grand-pianos' of yew frame vistas and give architectural structure.

garden feature it has a distinctive character. Its design may either be worked out according to some strict geometric formula (with straight or curved lines) or may follow some asymmetrical plan. The maze at GLENDURGAN planted in 1833 is a good example of a design of the latter kind – well chosen for its setting. It is made of Cherry Laurel (*Prunus laurocerasus*), on a sloping site, and was intended to introduce a relatively formal note in the woodland setting of the exotic tender shrubs and trees that surround it. A maze usually consists of a tortuous path, with many deceptive blind-alleys, through which one makes one's way to some specific destination, more often than not at its centre. Modern mazes are generally of two kinds. A turf maze is essentially two-dimensional and very much simpler to make one's way about than in mazes of hedging. Mazes of tall hedges, deciduous or evergreen, are easy to get lost in. Indeed, some old mazes thoughtfully have raised observation points – partly so that one can admire the pattern and partly so that one may shout directions to lost friends.

The word parterre means in French literally 'on the ground'. The parterre is a symmetrically arranged level bed in which clipped box or yew normally plays an important part. Topiary, statues, urns and water features of various kinds are often incorporated. The parterre is usually placed close to the house and firmly related to it. It is the essential ingredient in classical French gardens, and it became a common garden feature all over Europe in the seventeenth and eighteenth centuries and, in England, was revived in the Victorian period during which it became a craze. These Victorian parterres used massed summer annuals to form blocks of colour such as are seen today at PITMEDDEN. An elaboration of the parterre is the *parterre de broderie* (embroidered parterre) in which flowing, scroll-like patterns are formed of very low hedges generally of clipped small-leaved box or of *Santolina*.

Parterres and knot gardens are both highly artificial garden devices. Their relationship with the less formal

The box-edged compartments of the parterres de broderie *at Pitmedden are filled with massed single-colour blocks of summer annuals.*

parts of the garden needs careful working out. The usual arrangement is to have the parterre or knot very emphatically alongside the house and separated from the countryside by increasingly less formal features or completely isolated from it by walls or hedges. In classical French gardens Le Nôtre would have parterres of greater simplicity the further one progressed along the central vista, away from the house. For example, the most elaborate *parterre de broderie* would usually be immediately below the windows of the grand rooms of the house – as they are at both Versailles and Vaux-le-Vicomte. Such positioning is a general rule of garden design that makes much sense and applies to the choice of ornamental plants as well as to the structural elements.

These, then, are some of the ways in which patterned structure is given to the garden. The amateur gardener, owner of a small plot, should not be daunted when visiting a great garden, with its perfection of upkeep and dazzling borders. All great gardens embody principles from which the owner of the smallest garden may learn. Simplicity, and economy of effect, are probably the two most important lessons of all.

Clipped apple-trees make an unconventional but effective hedging material at The Courts. Their decorative flowers add interest in the spring and contrast with the bronze-tinted young foliage of the yew hedge and orange-yellow striped tulips.

HEDGES

Alexander Pope, writing about gardens, stressed the importance of variety, surprise and the concealment of bounds. Many gardeners would think of these as essential ingredients of their garden, and hedges are by far the best way of providing them. They are the living bones of a garden. As boundaries, internal walls, passages, windbreaks, buttresses or low edgings, they are the most essential of garden ingredients. Many different kinds of woody plants are suitable for hedging, and a guide to them appears at the end of the book.

The first hedges were almost certainly stock-proof field hedges. In England these are of very great antiquity – some have been reliably dated as more than a thousand years old. Early writings on farming are full of advice on hedge-making – 'Gette thy quickesettes in the woode-countreye, and let theym be of whytethorne and crab-tree . . . holye and hassell be goode' (*Fitzherbert's Book of Husbandry*, 1523). One of the earliest practical manuals of gardening, Thomas Hill's *The Gardener's Labyrinth* (1577) describes an ingenious method of making hedges by twisting hawthorn seeds into wet rope. When the seeds have germinated the rope is then buried where you want your hedge to run.

Before the Renaissance, hedges were a rarity in gardens – they were normally enclosed with walls, fences, trellis or palisades. In the seventeenth and early eighteenth centuries fashionable garden designs were based on the ideal of

At Crathes Castle enticing alleys between ramparts of yew, planted in 1702, show the powerful structural presence of old hedges.

the Italian Renaissance gardens, where a series of outside 'rooms' were linked together and to the house by pathways and terraces and by steps between different levels. Hedging plants and walls built of local brick or stone were used to make these divisions. In England this idea of the garden built up of compartments was universal until the sweeping changes of the eighteenth-century landscape movement. It is a principle to which we returned in the latter half of the nineteenth century and has been the ruling style in many of the great gardens of the twentieth century.

In the country the most satisfactory perimeter hedges blend harmoniously with the surrounding landscape. Six British natives, all common hedgerow plants of ancient use, are often and successfully used: hawthorn (also known as quickthorn and may), beech, hornbeam, holly, Field Maple and barberry.

Hawthorn (*Crataegus monogyna*), the commonest field hedge in England, makes a beautiful boundary. In some country places it is still meticulously 'laid'; this involves partly severing the trunks, bending them over and tying them to vertical stakes. The glossy lobed leaves cover it densely, and the flowers have a delicious scent. It also has decorative crimson haws in the autumn, though these, alas, will be scarce on a tightly clipped hedge since the best time for clipping is after flowering. To ensure the presence of at least a few fruits, one should clip the hedge gently, leaving much of the older growth. Such a hedge, with its less crisply defined shape, may, furthermore, be more appropriate in an informal position. At ERDDIG hawthorn is used to excellent effect to enclose the orchard that lies to one side of the outhouses. In this rural setting the magnificent 3.6m/12ft hawthorn hedge, with the slightly pink new growth speckled with flowers in spring, provides a perfect background.

Beech (*Fagus sylvatica*), which keeps some of its attractive russet leaves in the winter, fits the country scene very well. With clipping it forms a dense, twiggy mass which even in winter provides effective protection from cold winds. Beech hedges in rural places look better with a curved top rather than a square-cut one. Beech is found as an internal, dividing, hedge in many gardens – for example at HIDCOTE and at LEVENS HALL, where 300-year-old beech hedges are one of the glories of the garden. At DUNHAM MASSEY an old hedge of Copper Beech fell into neglect and has now become a grove of trees 9m/30ft high.

Hornbeam (*Carpinus betulus*) has much in common with beech (including the characteristic of keeping its dead leaves – which turn yellow – in the winter). If anything, its leaf is more elegant than that of beech – but of a slightly duller green. John Evelyn thought hornbeam made 'the noblest and stateliest hedge for long walks in

'Cottage-loaves' of two different kinds of holly make an appropriate and original hedge in the wild garden at The Courts.

gardens or parks because it grows tall and so sturdy as not to be wronged by the winds.' The hornbeam walk at HIDCOTE corresponds to this description. Hornbeam also has the advantage over beech that it is much more likely to 'break' from old wood if drastic cutting back is needed.

Holly (*Ilex aquifolium*) is at its best as a perimeter hedge. It is one of the handsomest evergreens with its glossy deep-green foliage and forms an impenetrable barrier; John Evelyn describes it vividly 'glittering with its armed and varnished leaves.' Within the garden, hand-weeding near a holly hedge is a painful business and one of the round-leaved forms of holly is a better choice. At THE COURTS there is a charming and unusual holly hedge used at the eastern boundary of the wild garden to the south of the main lawn. Here two kinds of holly are grown together – Common Holly (*I. aquifolium*) and its cultivar 'J. C. van Tol' which has much larger oblong leaves with fewer spikes than the type. The hedge is clipped into a series of cottage-loaf shapes, and it is an excellent example of an appropriate hedging material treated in an imaginative but unsophisticated way.

Field Maple (*Acer campestre*) is a quick-growing deciduous tree with many virtues as a hedging plant. It has very attractive foliage, tinged with pink in the spring before turning to a good fresh green. In autumn it turns a dazzling yellow. At TINTINHULL it makes an eloquent link between the countryside and the formal garden.

Barberry (*Berberis vulgaris*) makes a beautiful and unusual hedge. It is extremely vigorous, has most attractive racemes of yellow flowers in May and stunning egg-shaped scarlet berries in autumn. In many ways it is even more beautiful than its flashier cousins that are the pride of the mixed border. It is not found (and should not be planted) in areas of predominantly arable farming as it is host to a virulent disease called Wheat Rust.

A mixture of several different plants can make an exceptionally attractive hedge. At BARRINGTON COURT, facing the orchard, there is a 1.5m/5ft high hedge of Field

Low hedges of copper-beech flank a path in the kitchen garden at Barrington Court. Shallow borders of red and pink penstemons vivify the sombre foliage of the beech and harmonise with the pink of brick walls and basket-weave paths.

At Westbury Court a viewing pavilion commands the head of the Long Canal which ends in a clairvoyée
*pierced in the brick wall. The elegant formality is continued in the flanking yew hedges with their finials of yew
cones and holly spheres.*

Maple, hornbeam, beech (common and copper) and the decorative Myrobalan or Cherry Plum (*Prunus cerasifera*). Hedges of contrasting foliage can introduce a lively note in more formal schemes. In the Fuchsia Garden at HIDCOTE there are hedges of holly and Copper Beech. The sparkle of the holly-leaf enlivens the sombre beech. Also at Hidcote, in the round 'green room', the yew hedges have contrasting patches of box at regular intervals.

Another native, yew (*Taxus baccata*), the grandest of all hedging materials, is emphatically *not* for the perimeter in the country. It is poisonous to livestock and should in no circumstances be planted where it may be grazed.

In general, perimeter hedges in country gardens are best kept simple and unadorned. This is usually not the best place for crenellations and curlicues which may well find a place within the garden. The appearance of the perimeter in relation to the surrounding country needs careful thought – and discretion – for it marks the point where nature ends and garden begins. In town or suburban gardens – or for the internal compartments of larger country gardens – a more elaborate hedge, of fancier material, is perfectly appropriate.

Within the garden the range of appropriate hedging plants is enormous. The choice will, to some extent, be dictated by the site. Yew, for example, dreads a waterlogged position. In warmer areas, with tender plants such as Holm Oak or myrtle, you will need a generally warm garden and a position protected from icy blasts. At MOUNT STEWART, which has an exceptionally mild climate, there are successful low hedges of – among other plants – rue (*Ruta graveolens* 'Jackman's Blue') and *Santolina (S. chamae-cyparissus)*. There the colour of the hedge is carefully related to adjacent plantings. Some forms of conifers have a strongly glaucous or yellow leaf colour difficult to harmonize with other colours. Details of the characteristics of different plants are given in the list at the end of the book.

Two plants, yew and box, stand out as exceptionally

Long-lived box in time assumes ungovernable shapes. At Barrington Court an old box hedge echoes the billowing outline of the border facing it.

versatile – combining most of the ideal qualities of garden hedging. They are both evergreen, perfectly hardy in the British Isles, immensely long-lived, take clipping very well and form a dense texture of great beauty that provides a perfect background to plants. To this formidable catalogue of virtues must be added, in the case of box, the irresistible scent of its leaves. Yew is of very ancient garden use and is found listed in some of the earliest catalogues of monastic plants. The monk Aelfric, for example, grew it in 995 – its branches were used as 'palm fronds' in religious ceremonies. For hedges, however, its use is much more recent. John Evelyn seems to have popularized it. In his book *Sylva* (1664) he says, 'I do name them [i.e. yews] for hedges, preferable for beauty and a stiff defence, to any plant I have ever seen and may . . . without vanity be said to have been the first who brought it into fashion.' Among the oldest yew hedges in Britain are the superb ones planted in 1702 at CRATHES CASTLE.

Today, yew is a vital ingredient in many outstanding gardens where its rich, dark green foliage has immense distinction. It has the reputation for being slow-growing.

On a steep slope the pattern of beds at Upton House is emphasised by the muscular outlines of the yew hedges that surround them.

In fact, correctly planted and properly fed, it will easily put on 300mm/1ft a year. A ten-year-old hedge is already making a major contribution to the appearance of a garden, and by the time it is fifteen years old it will seem as though it has always been there. There are other evergreens that will grow more quickly but none that, in the end, will provide a hedge of such beauty. Nor is very vigorous growth necessarily an advantage in plants for hedging. Yew needs clipping only once a year.

Old yew is remarkably robust and at many National Trust gardens the regeneration or reshaping of yews has been very successfully carried out. Even with annual clipping hedges still gradually increase their size. The increase is so gradual as to be invisible except over a long period of time. A yew hedge at CLIVEDEN on either side of the entrance to the forecourt, planted in the early eighteenth century had, by the 1980s, grown 9m/30ft wide and about the same in height. It had become completely out of scale with its elegant surroundings and has now been reduced to a height of 3.6m/12ft and a width of 1.5m/5ft. Hedges may also need cutting back when they begin to

obstruct passages. At POWIS CASTLE the hedge running along the south-east end of the old kitchen gardens had become much too broad for the raised terrace on which it is planted. All the growth on that side was cut right back to the trunk, from which new growth has vigorously sprouted. Some hedges have suffered unavoidable neglect, for example as a result of labour shortage during the Second World War. Neglected hedges have been very successfully reformed at POWIS CASTLE, HARDWICK HALL and KINGSTON LACY.

In theory the best time to cut yews back in this way is in late winter or early spring. In practice, in National Trust gardens, major operations of this sort are carried out when the gardening staff have enough time to do them properly. The autumn, when in any case the yews may be receiving their annual trim, is often a convenient time because the pressure of other work is not so great. Yews *must* be in good health before cutting back. As a first step the top of the hedge should be taken off as well as one side. Any ivy, which stifles new growth, should be removed. After 'stumping' some extra nourishment should be given. Vitax Q4 is an effective and very widely used form. The fuzz of new growth that quickly appears in the spring is rather vulnerable to scorching when the sun is hot, but no permanent damage is caused. To allow the plants to regain their strength, three years should be allowed between stumping each side. After about eight years, with regular doses of fertilizer, the hedge will be in fine fettle. Irish Yews (*Taxus baccata* 'Fastigiata') respond equally well to cutting back. At ERDDIG an avenue of old Irish Yews had become excessively blowsy and misshapen. They were cut down in the winter of 1975/6 to 600mm/2ft stumps from which they have quickly formed handsome new shapes. The National Trust has found, however, that stumping of yews does not seem to work so well in Yorkshire and further north where it has lost at least 50 per cent of yews treated in this way.

The golden form of yew (*T. b. aurea*) is a tricky

The richly-planted beds at Plas-yn-Rhiw are given structural patterning by the network of yew hedges that encloses the garden compartments. In this seaside garden the hedges also provide wind shelter for the tender plants that thrive there.

At Erddig large old Irish yews, grown too big and shapeless, were cut back to 600mm/2ft stumps from which they naturally formed the shapely outlines shown here. The yews are fringed with a low key-pattern box hedge and a corresponding row of pyramid-trained apple trees.

customer. I find it often appears excessively shrill, but on a dull day it can add liveliness to an otherwise sombre scene. In the forecourt at POLESDEN LACEY simple clipped mounds of it edge the perimeter, and at WIGHTWICK MANOR it is used effectively in the formal gardens to make giant clipped drums. At LEVENS HALL some of the topiary is of golden yew which, on a sunless day, gives the curious optical illusion of a single ray of light illuminating it. Golden Yew can, of course, be successfully regenerated

by stumping back, as has been shown at SHUGBOROUGH.

Box (*Buxus sempervirens*) is another immensely valuable hedging plant. It is less vigorous than yew and is most frequently seen as a low hedge. At MOTTISFONT ABBEY it is used with telling effect in the former vegetable garden which now houses a remarkable collection of old roses. The firm lines of the beautifully clipped box hedges which edge all the paths introduce discipline to the unconstrained shapes of the shrub roses and also conceal their ungainly lower branches. Box can make a very high hedge indeed. At POWIS CASTLE there are magnificent box hedges 5.4m/18ft high lining a path to one side of the terraces. It is the most versatile of all edging plants either in its common form or as the small-leaved cultivar (*B. s.* 'Suffruticosa'). There are several other cultivars with gold, variegated or glaucous leaves. Even in the case of the type, the size and colour of leaf varies considerably, and if uniformity is important, it is essential to obtain vegetatively propagated plants from the same source. Unlike yew, box does not generally respond well to drastic cutting back. At CLIVEDEN the old box hedging of the parterre on the south side of the house had become extremely misshapen. This was cut back fairly roughly to its correct dimensions. About 75 per cent of the plants survived and replacements were planted in the gaps. It has taken ten years to achieve a reasonable appearance. The Head Gardener at Cliveden, Mr Philip Cotton, believes that it is more satisfactory to cut box down to a stump of about 150mm/6in. He did this with the box edging in the Long Garden at Cliveden and, although full recovery took ten years, the results are excellent. Box also seems to transplant quite successfully. At TATTON PARK some unusual large-leaved golden box plants, over one hundred years old, were recently transplanted satisfactorily from the nineteenth-century Italian parterres to edge the paths in the former kitchen garden.

PLANTING A HEDGE

With any large hedge the preparation of the ground is of the greatest importance. It may sound like a great chore, and indeed it is, but it is worth remembering that the health, vigour and beauty of the hedge – which may easily last your lifetime – could depend on it. The hedge will also become established much more quickly if the ground is properly prepared. Plants in hedges are expected to grow very vigorously and thus need an exceptionally favourable environment to flourish. Thorough preparation of the ground will encourage the roots of each plant to go deeper

Box is rarely allowed to grow to its maximum height. At Powis Castle there is an exceptional old box hedge which now stands 5.4m/18ft high.

in search of nourishment – and not compete with those of its neighbour. For all large hedging plants, roughly speaking all those which would grow into trees, a trench 1m/3ft wide and 600mm/2ft deep should be made and all perennial weeds carefully removed. The top spit should be put on one side and as much compost or rotted manure as you can find (at least one bucket per square metre/yard) worked into the lower spit, breaking it up if necessary with a pick-axe. The top spit can then be replaced. If you do not take this trouble and if subsequently your hedge sulks horribly, you will always regret having been lazy.

The spacing of different plants is dealt with in the list at the end of the book. As a general principle shallow-rooted plants should be fairly well spaced out – 900mm/3ft is not too much for yew. If they are placed too close together their roots will be in competition for nourishment; the hedge will initially grow perfectly well, but as soon as the roots overlap with each other, will start to languish. In general it is better to use young plants. Yew, for example, 300mm/1ft high is quite big enough. It is also worth mentioning that if yew plants are planted in poorly drained ground or deeper than they were in the nursery – even 12mm/½in deeper – then they can turn brown, which is a sure sign of failure. The plants may seem puny little things and your hedge very unhedge-like but the small plants have great advantages. First, they transplant much better than larger plants and therefore establish themselves more painlessly. Secondly they will not need the support that larger plants will. This is especially important in exposed sites (where you may most want to plant a hedge) where firm staking of each plant will add immensely to the work and expense.

It is essential, if you want a hedge of uniform appearance, that the plants should have been propagated vegetatively from the same source or that young plants are very carefully matched. Plants propagated from cuttings will often continue the habit of growth of the exact part of the parent plant from which they were taken. (For example, yew propagated from side roots may well show a distressing yearning for the horizontal life.) However, mixed hedges can be made of chance seedlings dug up in your garden – yew and holly seem to self-sow in the most obliging way. Variations in leaf-colour and form will be part of the attraction of such a hedge. At WESTBURY COURT yew hedges flanking either side of the canal show considerable variation in colour, which adds greatly to their charm.

In the past it was common to plant hedges with a staggered double row of plants. This is rarely done today, partly because it makes weeding very difficult and partly because the plants will be in even greater competition with each other for available nourishment. One of the reasons for planting in this way was to make a thick hedge quickly. Sometimes as a consequence these hedges were not sufficiently cut back early in their lives and thus no dense framework of branches and thick trunk were formed. This can cause problems later if it is necessary to cut hedges back severely. In addition, with staggered or double rows of plants, the two sides of a hedge can lean away from each other making tall hedges impossibly wide and difficult to maintain. At MOTTISFONT ABBEY the box hedges of the south parterre and the yew hedges at the entrance to the lime walk are planted in staggered double rows and the growth of the trunks is too spindly to take drastic cutting back.

Today virtually all plants for hedges are sold in containers. It is a good idea to buy from a nursery specializing in hedging, where propagation is more likely to have been done from good stock. If you buy plants from a garden centre make sure that, especially with the less popular varieties, they have not become root-bound in their containers. If they have, they will take a long time to become established.

Plants should be planted at the same depth as they were at the nursery and should be well firmed in. Smallish plants will need no support but in very exposed areas plastic mesh fixed to bamboos will soften the impact of wind until they are well established.

In the summer after planting – and subsequent summers when young – do not forget to water a new hedge copiously in dry weather. Young plants in newly dug earth (which has better drainage) are very vulnerable to drought. Weeding a newly planted hedge is also vital. Weeds compete for nourishment and moisture and make the hedge look very untidy. As the hedge thickens out weeds will become less frequent as seeds fail to germinate in the dry shade .

Powis Castle is one of the few great formal gardens to have survived the eighteenth-century craze for landscaping. The south-facing early eighteenth-century terraces have ancient ramparts of yew which rise in some places to 15m/50ft.

Box topiary at Hidcote Manor provides pattern and structure in the White Garden. The shapes link with the arched entrances of yew and in high summer make a disciplined framework for the exuberant herbaceous planting below.

MAINTENANCE

Clipping and feeding are the two most important aspects of hedge maintenance. Initial clipping will be done chiefly to establish the shape of the hedge and to ensure the correct growth of each plant. The top growth on young plants should not be clipped until the desired height is achieved. The side growth should be firmly clipped – both to shape the hedge and to encourage vigorous and uniform growth. The harder you clip back the more growth will be stimulated at that point.

It used to be a general principle of shaping tall hedges that a 'batter' should be established; that is to say the base of the hedge should be wider than the top. The reason for this is to allow light to reach all parts of the hedge evenly. If the base is deprived of light the growth will become straggly. In addition a dense evergreen hedge with a narrow top and sloping sides will be much less likely to be harmed by a heavy snowfall. Nathaniel Lloyd in his excellent book *Garden Craftsmanship in Yew and Box* says that for a yew hedge the batter should be 50-100mm/2-4in for every 300mm/1ft of height. This would mean that a 1.8m/6ft high hedge that is 750mm/30in across at the base should be 150-450mm/6-18in across at the top. That is a counsel of perfection. One very rarely sees yew hedges with a pronounced batter – most, indeed, have none at all.

A horizontal line is helpful to keep straight when clipping the tops of smaller hedges such as box. With larger hedges it is easier to keep straight and level and irregularities are less obvious. The great yew hedge that runs along the western edge of the canal terrace at BODNANT is 90m/300ft long and is not only clipped entirely by eye, but is also clipped by hand.

Clipping may be done with hand shears, secateurs or mechanical clippers. It is important, for both the appearance and the health of hedges, that shears should be kept as sharp as possible. Blunt shears will mangle the leaves, especially broad leaves. The effect of the damage may not be immediately visible but will rapidly become so as the damaged leaves turn brown and start to die back. Some broad-leaved hedges, for example Portugal Laurel or bay, are, in any case, better shaped with secateurs, removing individual branches rather than clipping the leaves. For large expanses of hedging, for example of yew, mechanical clippers are almost universally used. One exception already mentioned is that of Bodnant, where Mr Martin Puddle, the Head Gardener, is quite insistent that clipping with hand shears is the only satisfactory technique, giving a much denser and firmer surface to a hedge. At TATTON PARK the Head Gardener, Mr Sam Youd, not only clips by hand but insists that it takes no longer than by machine. Elsewhere in National Trust and other large gardens machine clipping is very widely used although fine detail (such as in topiary) is frequently done with hand shears. The most commonly used machine is the Little Wonder electric trimmer with reciprocal action blades. It may be plugged directly into the mains or, more conveniently, have its own generator and thus can be used anywhere in the garden. It is also, in its smaller (450mm/18in) size, relatively light. The time of year to clip a hedge is given in the directory at the end of the book; the important principle is *not* to clip when it looks as though frost is possible.

Clipping very tall hedges or topiary can present problems of access. At POWIS CASTLE the ancient ramparts of yew are so high that a triple-section (15m/50ft) ladder is needed to scale the top. Scaffolding towers on wheels are widely used, but these can be difficult to manoeuvre in narrow spaces. At Levens Hall the great 300-year-old beech hedges, 4.5m/15ft high and as much wide are now clipped with the help of aluminium trestles on wheels, joined over the top of the hedge by a stout aluminium platform. But among the topiary at Levens only small trestles and ladders are possible. HIDCOTE has a wealth of topiary and four miles of hedging which, because of densely planted borders and narrow openings, is fairly inaccessible. There is no room to manoeuvre large trestles, and ladders are used. In gardens such as PACKWOOD HOUSE with many very large topiary specimens, access is easier and clipping is done with the help of a dumper truck with a hydraulic arm and a platform which is hired every year. At LANHYDROCK the twenty-nine Irish Yews in the formal garden are now 7.5m/25ft high and 3m/10ft in diameter at their bases. These are such a vital feature and their maintenance so important that the garden has bought its own Hy-Lift T95 hydraulic lift which allows the yews to be clipped in three-and-a-half days. It will extend to a maximum height of 9.6m/32ft and is thus also very valuable for the maintenance of trees in the woodland garden. Other gardens, such as HIDCOTE, where such a piece of equipment would be of immense use, the trees are unfortunately just too densely planted to allow easy manoeuvring.

Beech hedges (left) at Hidcote Manor provide a distinguished contrast to the alley of hornbeam – which has a similar but subtly different foliage.

Many gardeners with small to medium-sized gardens use small electric hedge-trimmers which plug into the mains. With serpentine lengths of flex trailing about it is remarkably easy to get into a tangle and even to cut the flex. This is extremely dangerous and can be fatal. There is a special plug on the market known as a current breaker (or, more impressively, a Residual Current Device) which in the event of accidentally cutting the flex instantly switches off the supply. It is inexpensive and very well worth buying and leaving permanently attached to the extension lead that you use with the trimmer or with any other electrical garden tool. Hedge-trimmers vary considerably in their safety, and accidents are common. The commonest involves stretching out with one hand to move a branch while holding the trimmer, still running, with the other. Some will not operate unless they are held with both hands. Some also have a quick-stop switch that stops the blades moving instantly. Others have extensions that shield the cutting blades making it more difficult to cut oneself accidentally. It is worth looking for all these features when choosing a trimmer.

Also available is a chemical (dikegulac-sodium; a common brand in Britain is ICI Cutlass) that retards the growth of the leading shoots and stimulates side growth. It should be sprayed on after clipping in a dilution that varies with the species of plant. It is not recommended for some plants (e.g. yew and box), and it cannot be used on hedges less than three years old. I find the very idea of such chemical interference with the growth of plants perfectly horrible. Others may decide that the expense and trouble of applying the chemical is not worth the candle. But it certainly works and some adventurous hi-tech gardeners with fast-growing evergreen hedges will pounce on it with cries of delight.

However well-prepared the soil, a new hedge will still need feeding. Every time you clip a hedge you are depriving it of part of its nutritive system. A mulch of well-rotted farmyard manure is best of all – suppressing

The belvedere at Claremont approached up a grassy slope flanked by hedges of beech – here showing fine autumn colour.

weeds and providing the humus-making conditions. Failing this, some proprietary make of slow-release fertilizer forked into the surface each year in the spring is a help. In extremely old hedges it is sometimes, because the shallow roots have grown great distances to some inaccessible spot, rather difficult to provide nourishment. For example, at CRATHES two years ago the Head Gardener, Mr David Maclean, noticed that lichen was beginning to appear on the wood of the huge yew hedges which had been planted in 1702. This was taken to be a sign that nourishment was needed. As an experiment, in the winter of 1987/8, 300mm/1ft squares of turf were removed at 600mm/2ft intervals in six staggered rows 600mm/2ft apart in the lawn on one side of one hedge starting at a distance of 3m/10ft. Holes 600mm/2ft deep were made with a crowbar and filled with a mixture of compost and Vitax VN2 (a slow-release fertilizer) and the turf replaced.

This seemed already to be having a beneficial effect in the summer of 1988. In other gardens where yews are planted in turf, such as at PACKWOOD HOUSE, it is thought that the yews, whose roots run below the lawns, receive all the extra nourishment they need from annual dressings of lawn fertilizer. An alternative is to use a foliar feed but this, unless repeated frequently, provides only a fleeting boost. The National Trust finds that most of the problems with hedges and topiary occur when they are surrounded by lawns. In this setting aeration, drainage and feeding can all cause difficulties. The first two are particular problems where large numbers of visitors cause compaction of the soil. At Packwood many yews were approaching death until drainage and surface aeration were improved. In such positions, good maintenance of turf (drainage, aeration and feeding) generally ensures healthy hedges and topiary.

LINES OF INFLUENCE

Pleaching, Arbours, Pergolas and Tunnels, Trellis and Avenues

In this chapter I shall be dealing with structural garden features – other than hedges – that are made from plants and with those that serve as decorative or structural supports for plants. Most of them have in common a linear emphasis and versatility in giving height in a decorative way and will contribute decisively to a garden's character.

PLEACHING

Pleaching – or plashing as it is sometimes known – means intertwining. A plashed hedge is one in which branches have been bent down and interwoven to form an impenetrable barrier. This very ancient technique was known to the Romans and mentioned by Julius Caesar who saw it used as a military obstacle in Flanders. In gardens, too, it has a long history. In *Much Ado about Nothing* Shakespeare refers to 'Walking in a thick pleached alley in my orchard'.

Pleaching today involves intertwining the upper branches of a series of regularly spaced trees leaving the lower trunks bare. A pleached hedge is a structural feature of special virtues. It has the advantage of making a screen – yet it does not obscure completely what lies beyond it. Thus it can mark out a part of the garden without isolating it from the rest or sheltering a path, perhaps as a calm transitional interval between different parts of the garden.

Screens of pleached lime (Tilia × euchlora) have been used effectively at Erddig to take the place of brick walls in the restoration of the original eighteenth-century layout.

One of the best examples of pleaching is the 'stilt garden' at HIDCOTE which is made of hornbeam (*Carpinus betulus*). Lawrence Johnston, who made the garden at Hidcote, was born in France and much influenced by French formal garden devices. This particular type of pleached alley is a *palissade à l'italienne*. At Hidcote it takes the form of a pair of double rows of trees whose trunks are bare to a height of 1.8m/6ft and the foliage has been trained and clipped into a solid block above. The alley is surfaced in gravel with a grass path down the middle. The turf is slightly raised with brick edging and where it protrudes just beyond each end of the alley the apron is curved forward in an inviting way. In summer the luxuriant and dense foliage with its attractive colour casts deep, cooling shade. In the winter, with only a few dead leaves remaining, the structure is still firmly visible – an intricate twiggy mass. It is trimmed in late summer and has been successfully rejuvenated by cutting back by 450mm/18in inside and out.

Hornbeam, unlike beech, responds well to very hard cutting back. New wires were fixed to train the resulting vigorous new growth. In the past this pleached alley was fed by a most elaborate procedure. The gravel was scraped away and manure was heaped up and left as a nutritive mulch from October to April. It was then removed and the gravel raked back into place. Feeding trees set in gravel is a problem, and at Hidcote the Head Gardener, Mr Paul Nicholls, is exploring the use of foliar feeds. But this may provide only a momentary boost when what is really needed in old plants of this sort is long-term nourishment to the roots.

*In the walled garden at Buscot Park an unusual alley of
pleached hop hornbeam* (Ostrya carpinifolia) *is underplanted
with day-lilies.*

At BUSCOT PARK a new walk of pleached Hop Hornbeam (*Ostrya carpinifolia*) is being made in the walled garden. This tree closely resembles Hornbeam but has the additional attraction, on the male plants, of decorative hop-like fruit in autumn. The walk goes right across the garden, following the curve of the round pool at the centre. The trees are planted 2.7m/9ft apart with bare trunks up to 2.1m/7ft. Aluminium crosspieces 900mm/3ft long, linked by wire, have been fixed to train the growth into a solid hedge-shape. In the beds that run along the trees, an especially imaginative and effective planting of shallow-rooted plants begins in spring with a lavish mixture of the White Grape Hyacinth *Muscari botryoides album*, mixed colours of *Anemone blanda*, *Crocus speciosus* 'Aitchisonii' and 'Conqueror', and tulips 'Black Parrot', 'White Triumphator' and *T. praestans* 'Fusilier'. This is followed in summer by alliums – *AA. aflatunense*, *giganteum* and *rosenbachianum* and waves of day-lilies, over fifty different cultivars from ANTONY HOUSE, ranging in colour from lemon-yellow to deep red. This dense planting needs regular feeding to look at its best; in spring and at midsummer Growmore is raked in. At right angles to the Hop Hornbeam alley is the interesting experiment of a walk of pleached Judas Trees (*Cercis siliquastrum*). The Judas Tree produces its pink-purple flowers on naked wood in early summer. It really needs a warm climate to flower well and in England only does so after a very hot summer. The slightly glaucous, rounded leaves are most decorative.

Lime trees are among the commonest materials for pleaching. The Common Lime (*Tilia × europaea*) is not the best for this purpose as it is very prone to suckering which spoils the clean lines of the trunks. In addition, it is susceptible to attacks from aphids which deposit a soot-like film of honeydew on the leaves. A better choice is the Broad-leaved Lime *T. platyphyllos*, the attractive pale-green leaves of which flutter slightly in a breeze giving a welcome sense of movement. This movement provides an effective contrast to the linear formality of an alley. At THE COURTS the entrance path is lined with a pleached alley of *Tilia platyphyllos*, making a firm and peaceful counterpoint to the rather frenzied late Georgian ornament of the house. The only problem about this tree is that its flowers open in late July, much later than other limes, and are narcotic to bees which may be found lurking, drowsy but dangerous, round about. With pleaching this will not necessarily be a problem as there will not be many flowers. Another lime that has been frequently used for ornamental purposes is *Tilia × euchlora* with smaller, more strikingly heart-shaped leaves. Unfortunately this lime is susceptible to a bacterial disease called Slime Flux, and the National Trust have found that half of the major garden features (avenues and pleached hedges) in which it has been used have been killed in the last few years and it is expected that the remainder will suffer.

Making a pleached screen or alley is not difficult. The first essential is a solid and long-lasting superstructure of uprights and horizontal wires. The uprights should be of hardwood or of some pressure-treated softwood. The upright at each end should be additionally supported with an angle-brace. Standard trees of 1.5-1.8m/5-6ft high should be used and planted 3m/10ft apart. The ground should be prepared thoroughly with plenty of compost worked into the lower level.

If planting in turf, square planting holes seem to look better than round ones and should be cut at least 600mm/2ft square. (Incidentally, the humus-rich turf, if chopped and incorporated into the bottom layer of the planting hole, can be a useful source of nourishment.) The horizontal wires, which are needed to shape the framework of interwoven branches, should be stretched at not less than 300mm/1ft intervals between upright supports to whatever height you desire – less than 2.4m/8ft looks a bit skimpy. Depending on the height of the uprights their bases should be firmly embedded in holes

The broad-leaved lime (Tilia platyphyllos) *makes an effective pleached alley linking the entrance gate to the front door of The Courts.*

Rudyard Kipling laid out the garden for Bateman's, his Sussex house. Screens of pleached lime attractively divide space and make architectural links with the house. Keeping trunks bare allows glimpses of other parts of the garden.

600-900mm/2-3ft deep with rubble and cement. The best way of keeping the wire taut is to attach it to eyes with adjustable screws. This framework will probably be needed for many years so the materials should be chosen with care from the point of view of both beauty and strength. Angled metal uprights are occasionally used, as at ERDDIG, but I think they are very ugly. One day you may think that your pleaching looks so wonderfully solid that

you can safely remove the supports. Do not be in any hurry to do so. The large expanse of pleached branches makes a formidable wind-break which could easily be blown over.

The trunks of the young trees should be kept bare of branches to a height of at least 1.2m/4ft. Laterals should be firmly attached to the wires and any growth from the trunk that is in the wrong place removed.

ARBOURS

I take an arbour to be the same as a bower, a place for sitting, decoratively shaded with plants, a meaning it has had since the early eighteenth century. The meaning of the word arbour has changed. It used to mean a lawn – and this is still the primary meaning given in the *Oxford English Dictionary*. In the making of an arbour plants may take a greater or lesser part. We are concerned here with arbours in which plants play an essential role. Some arbours may be made entirely of trellis or other wood-work, or even fibreglass. One of the most satisfying forms is one in which plants with fragrant flowers or leaves are a principal ingredient: an arbour swathed in scented climb-ing roses can be wonderfully decorative and a delicious place to sit. One of the earliest paintings of an arbour, the *Histoire de Charles Martel* by Loyset Liédet (1470), shows a turf seat backed with profusely flowering white roses. Roses should be chosen that are not excessively vigorous and that can be pruned and tied in neatly. By choosing a few different varieties that flower in sequence it should be possible to maintain a flowery arbour over a long season.

As a way of displaying climbing plants to show their special virtues the arbour is very valuable. The new rose arbour at MOTTISFONT ABBEY, made in 1985, is a circle of elegant 2.4m/8ft high octagonal posts linked by metal hoops. The posts are oak and they are embedded in the concrete base of the arbour. The framework is of mild steel, primed and painted black. It has an emphatically late-Victorian or Edwardian air – entirely appropriate for the roses displayed on it, which date from that period. Trained up each post and over the hoops are Rambler roses of two different kinds, planted alternately: the pale rose-pink 'Debutante', whose vigour belies her rather demure name; and 'Bleu Magenta' with rich purple flowers. Between each pair of posts in a bed encircling the arbour, a specimen of the rose 'Little White Pet', trained as a standard, is underplanted with a froth of wormwood (*Artemisia absinthium* 'Lambrook Silver'). The wormwood

A simple metal arbour of sweet-peas in the walled garden of Crathes Castle forms a scented and decorative intersection of paths.

Lavender alleys lead up to the rose arbour at Mottisfont Abbey which is festooned with Rambler roses. Arbours not only give height but many provide a decorative sitting place and here make a shapely meeting point of several paths.

MOTTISFONT
Rose Arbour

Arches of flat iron 64 m × 10 mm (2½ × ⅜ in)

DIMENSIONS: *6.7m (22ft) in diameter*

Tapered octagonal hardwood posts

is proving too vigorous, rather swamping the delicate rose, and it is now proposed to substitute the much smaller *Artemisia canescens*. The outer edges of the border are planted with the pink *Dianthus* 'White Ladies' and dotted about within it is the rich, deep red old HT rose 'Marchioness of Salisbury'. In the middle of the arbour a rather lumpish flint-covered centrepiece is surrounded by a metal bench where one may sit, enveloped in sweet scents, and admire views of the rose garden framed in rosy arches.

The Rambler roses are severely pruned as soon as the last flowers fade. Where possible the previous year's stems are reduced to ground level, or to the lowest convenient point, to stimulate vigorous growth from the base and to discourage the formation of elderly, woody stems. Severe pruning of this sort is essential both to prevent the rose from overpowering the arbour and to encourage maximum flowering from the bottom upwards.

Throughout the remaining season new growth is trained in, and the roses are fed with a general fertilizer twice a year, in spring and summer immediately after pruning.

Arbours made of clipped plants with dense foliage allowing precise shaping can be most effective. At HESTERCOMBE in Somerset, a garden designed by Gertrude Jekyll and Edwin Lutyens, there is a powerfully architectural arbour made of trained and clipped Wych Elm (*Ulmus glabra*). It has a very deep, shady recess in which there is a bench, designed by Lutyens, echoing the shape of the arbour. Bench and arbour are precisely aligned with a 'rill' which flows towards the countryside beyond, an integral aspect of the garden design. At SHUGBOROUGH there is an ingenious flower-less arbour capitalizing on the naturally pendent habit of the Camperdown Elm (*Ulmus* 'Camperdownii'). It is loosely shaped round a metal framework – a great leafy hand cupping a garden seat.

In the walled rose garden at Polesden Lacey neat box hedges line the paths and make a linear contrast with the blowsy rambling roses.

Plants with good autumn colour make excellent decorative arbours. At CASTLE DROGO, there are giant arbours of Persian Ironwood (*Parrotia persica*) at each corner of the flower garden. They are boxed in with monumental walls of yew. In autumn the foliage colours spectacularly – leaves at the top of the tree turning a deep red and those farther down, yellow. The supporting posts of the arbours are planted in beds of a single plant, geraniums or Harts' Tongue Ferns, most effectively edged with the shiny ornamental leaves of *Asarum europaeum*.

PERGOLAS AND TUNNELS

Tunnels and pergolas are very similar. In the case of a tunnel the plants are so intertwined that in time they may provide their own support – they *become* the support. In a pergola the supports will usually be visible and may be very decorative in their own right. Perhaps somewhat arbitrarily, I also define pergolas as having square tops; tunnels, as the word suggests, having rounded ones. In many of the gardens designed by Gertrude Jekyll and Edwin Lutyens, pergolas were built with fastidious and

At Barrington Court a modern pergola benefits from a fine old path. Herbaceous plantings soften the crisp edges of the new brick pillars.

detailed attention to the quality and appropriateness of the material. These are sufficiently ornamental in themselves – the plants a wonderful bonus.

The word pergola comes from the Italian *pergula* which means a projection from a roof. One of the most ancient of garden features, pergolas were found in Pompeian frescos and were certainly known in the Middle Ages. Boccaccio vividly describes one in *The Decameron* (1358): 'All around the garden . . . ran wide walks covered with vines curved over . . . thus one is able to walk in a delightful, sweetly scented shade.' A tunnel of arcades in 'carpenter's work' is illustrated in the *Hypnerotomachia Poliphili* (1499), the earliest printed book to show ornamental gardens.

A pergola, as a design feature, may serve many purposes in a garden. It provides a decorative support for all kinds of climbing and twining plants. It may link different parts and provide a transitional interlude. In the heat of the summer it provides welcome shade ('this gallery of cool greenery' as Gertrude Jekyll described it) and possibly delicious scents from flowers at nose level. It affords views of other parts of the garden charmingly framed by the uprights swathed in diverse foliage.

It is worth remembering that plants grown on pergolas are much less protected than they are when grown against a wall. The more tender plants simply will not thrive on a very exposed pergola. Some pergolas, for example those at BODNANT and BARRINGTON COURT, are protected by walls or by closely planted shrubs and trees.

The new pergola built at BARRINGTON COURT in 1981 shows how versatile pergolas can be and how quickly they can have great decorative presence. It runs close to the wall on the south side of the part of the garden called the Beef Stalls. It is constructed of brick uprights, one-and-a-half bricks square and 2.4m/8ft high. The bricks are faced and had, when new, a rather harsh dark bluish-grey colour which did not harmonize at all with the surrounding ham-stone walls and old brick paths. The colour is now mellowed and the effect is not so starkly industrial as it was at first. The crosspieces are made of kapur, an African hardwood, and they are arranged in a criss-cross triangular pattern. Wires are stretched across to support the plants. The uprights are at 4.5m/15ft intervals. The path that runs between them is beautifully made of narrow bricks laid on their edges in basketweave patterns. The overall width of the pergola is 3m/10ft. Many spring- and summer-flowering plants are supported – clematis (*Clematis alpina* 'Frances Rivis', 'The President' and 'Hagley Hybrid'), honeysuckles (*Lonicera* × *tellmanniana* and *L. periclymenum* 'Serotina'), the Japanese *Wisteria floribunda*, the slightly tender *Solanum jasminoides* 'Album' and the herbaceous golden-leaved hop (*Humulus lupulus aureus*). The beds that run along either side of the path overflow with chiefly herbaceous plants which flourish in the semi-shade – hostas, hellebores, *Alchemilla mollis*, Solomon's Seal, *Pulmonaria* and *Euphorbia polychroma*. The wall backing it, which is north-facing and slightly higher than the pergola, is planted with cotoneasters (*CC. franchetii* and *horizontalis*), the self-clinging trumpet-vine

The generously wide pear tunnel at Bateman's leaves sufficient room for a contrasting planting of cranesbills, bergenias, lungwort, Solomon's seal and comfrey. Intertwined with the pears are clematis, honeysuckle and the rampant Cobaea scandens.

Campis radicans and *Chaenomeles speciosa* 'Moerloosei' whose pink-flushed white flowers resemble apple-blossom. The entrance to the west end is flanked by bushes of *Daphne odora* 'Aureo-marginata' whose spicily perfumed flowers provide in spring a deliciously scented prelude to the pergola. Maintenance consists of pruning the summer-flowering clematis in February and feeding the beds (with either Vitax Q4 or farmyard manure) in March, when slug pellets are put down to protect hostas. In the spring and summer new growth of the climbers is tied in. In late summer the honeysuckles are given a gentle shaping. Finally, in the autumn all dead herbaceous growth is removed.

The laburnum arch at BODNANT is a wonderfully instructive example of a carefully executed tunnel. It is an early feature of the garden, made by the present Lord Aberconway's great-grandfather in the 1880s, and some of the original plants survive. Laburnum, however, is not long-lived and there is continual replacement of the plants. It is over 70m/200ft long, 5m/15ft wide and 2.4m/8ft high. The sides slope very slightly inward and form a leisurely and graceful curve over the top. Incidentally, half-elliptical arches of this sort always seem much more satisfactory than half-round arches. The path curves very gently to follow the wall beside it. The framework is made of metal arches to which thin wooden laths are tied along the whole length of the tunnel. The plants now used are *Laburnum × watereri* 'Vossii' which has especially long racemes. They are planted at intervals of between 1-2m/3-6ft and the growth is fanned out to make a series of parallel branches running at right angles to the laths to which they are tied. The plants are staggered so that the growth on each side interlocks with that facing it. Each year the plants throw out vertical shoots up to 1.8m/6ft long on the top of the tunnel. In January three-quarters of these and any dead wood are pruned out. The remaining whippy growth is bent down and tied in. After flowering in late May or early June the dead flowers are removed.

The arched laburnum walk at Bodnant is uncontrived and spacious. Openings in the 'walls' afford glimpses of other parts of the garden.

Only occasional feeding is done – indeed, excessive vigour (and too much foliage at the expense of flowers) may be more of a problem than weak growth. The great charm of the Bodnant laburnum tunnel lies in subtle details. It is airily spacious and avoids an obvious straight line. It is edged with low dry-stone walls on which Welsh Poppies (*Meconopsis cambrica*) seed themselves among ferns and moss. Beyond the walls the rich planting of pink, red and purple azaleas fills the gaps between the laburnum trunks with spring colour.

Tunnels planted with fruit trees have a special character. Rudyard Kipling, an accomplished gardener, designed a striking tunnel of pears at BATEMAN'S, the house that he bought in Sussex in 1902. The pears – 'Conference', 'Doyenné du Comice' and 'Winter Nelis' – are all late-season, from late October to January, and the ripening fruit makes handsome winter decoration. A more

At Moseley Old Hall a tunnel of 'carpenter's work' is draped with grape-vines and clematis – leading to an enclosed formal topiary garden.

recent addition is the collection of summer-flowering clematises which follow the very decorative white pear blossom of the spring. Additional interest is provided by many bulbs and small herbaceous plants in the narrow (1.5m/5ft) beds that run along either side – daffodils, lungwort, bergenias, primroses and Corsican Hellebores. This tunnel is a dead-end – with a carefully shaped bench at its head which echoes the arch of the tunnel. The view from this seat is aligned with a doorway in the wall of the vegetable garden and a brick path that leads across the adjoining court. This careful siting gives the tunnel a satisfyingly purposeful air, carefully related to the structure of the garden.

The pleached Hornbeam tunnels at HAM HOUSE are reconstructions of historical features appropriate to the unusually complete seventeenth-century setting. They are designed also to make a 'viewing frame' for the knot garden. The tunnels lie on either side of the East Court knot. Hornbeams (*Carpinus betulus*) are pleached over an arched metal frame that rises to a maximum height of 2.4m/8ft. The plants are bare to a height of 1.8m/6ft. The 'walls' are formed by a continuous hedge of clipped yew 1.35m/4ft 6in high. Through the gap between yew and Hornbeam, attention is drawn to the striking knot that is spread out before it. These green tunnels, with their attractively contrasting foliage, very much resemble those seen in sixteenth-century paintings of Italian gardens. An essential point of such tunnels is the density and the evenness of the foliage. At Ham House the Hornbeam in the tunnels is pruned every year in January. New growth is removed to a leader which is tied in, making sure no growth overlaps. At LITTLE MORETON HALL a yew tunnel in a similar historic setting is being made to one side of the knot garden laid out in 1975. Here, a path 1.8m/6ft wide runs between metal hoops that rise to 2.1m/7ft high. Yews are planted at 600mm/2ft intervals and trained over the hoops. The yews are now being clipped, inside and out, to form smooth 'walls'.

A tunnel of limes at Hidcote Manor. Here, the young saplings were bent over and joined at the top, forming pointed arches.

Quite simple tunnels can be made by bending over the tops of plants until they meet. At HIDCOTE, a garden that contains many examples of handsome effects achieved with simplicity, there is a lime tunnel (planted by Lawrence Johnston) where the branches have been gently shaped into a Gothic ogee arch. This is clipped with secateurs in March and new growth is tied vertically on to horizontal wires fixed to the sturdier old plants. A similar effect is achieved at LYTES CARY where a double row of Hornbeams (*Carpinus betulus*) has been bent over to form a tunnel which leads through to an enclosed glade lightened by walls of *Weigela* 'Florida Variegata'. This tunnel is entered through a 'door' in a yew hedge, and the opening has been emphasized by being capped with a massive clipped Hornbeam lintel.

TRELLIS

The word trellis comes from the Latin *trilicius* which means woven together. It is a latticework of regularly spaced laths of wood forming either diamonds or squares. It can be used in many ways in the garden. At its simplest it is an easy way to heighten a wall and to provide a climbing-frame for plants. A more sophisticated use, increasingly popular today, is to make architectural

At Mottisfont Abbey, in the walled garden containing the National Collection of old roses, arches provide more vertical space for specimens.

shapes of it – archways, obelisks and so on. It can also be used, by creating false perspectives, to increase a feeling of space in a small area. Sometimes, unfortunately, it is used to impart a disagreeable atmosphere of twee-ness. Restraint, and firmness, should be the guides to its use.

Trellis has been used in the garden for a very long time. It was a common feature of Muslim gardens in southern Spain and is described in a remarkable early gardening book, Ibn Bassal's *The Book of Agriculture* (*c.* 1080) in which the author recommends trellis for jasmine and other plants. In the enclosed gardens of the Middle Ages it was used to divide the space and to support climbers. The miniatures of the *Très Riches Heures* of the Duc de Berry, painted in the early fifteenth century, illustrate it vividly. In France *treillage*, as it is called, became an essential part of the formal garden. By the early eighteenth century it had become so grand as to be suitable only for the smartest gardens, as Dézallier d'Argenville's *La Théorie et la Pratique du Jardinage* (1709) illustrates. It remains an attractive ingredient of French gardens, exemplified by the charming rose-covered trellis arbours in the *potager* at Villandry. In England trelliswork had become lavishly ornate by the beginning of the eighteenth century. Batty Langley's *New Principles of Gardening* (1728) illustrates some extraordinary architectural confections. With the revival of formal ideas in garden design in the nineteenth century it became fashionable once again. Trelliswork is fragile and few examples survive from the nineteenth century. Those that do, for example at TATTON PARK, need regular maintenance and replacement.

At BODNANT trellis is beautifully used both as fencing and as the superstructure for pergolas. Running along the edge of the lower rose terrace a 900mm/3ft high fence of trellis has ornamental onion-shaped finials on the uprights. Trained along the fence are *Clematis* 'Lasurstern' with deep-blue flowers, *C.* 'Marie Boisselot' with huge white flowers, *C. tangutica* with lemon-coloured hanging flowers and finely-cut foliage, and the climbing HT rose 'Cupid' with lemon-tinged pink flowers. At either end of the same terrace, and curving down the steps that lead down to it, are pergolas whose cross-pieces and supports are made of trellis. Originally these pergolas were painted rich blue/grey, which has faded over the years to a most attractive colour.

Trellis is used to embellish the mid-nineteenth-century Lady Charlotte's bower at TATTON PARK. It is made of lath-and-plaster and elegantly finished with trellis and flanked with wire filigree columns surmounted by open-work urns. Trained up either side of the bower is a climbing rose, the large-flowered creamy-yellow 'Paul's Lemon Pillar' and pale pink 'New Dawn'. Both are richly scented and in summer fill the bower with their fragrance. This bower is an original part of the nineteenth-century 'gardenesque' garden which it is hoped to restore soon to its former glory.

A lightly planted trellis fence makes an effective screen

At Lytes Cary, a tunnel of hornbeam leads out from an enclosed secret garden. The entrance is of clipped yew, topped by a hornbeam 'lintel'.

that still allows views of the garden beyond. At CRATHES trellis runs along the path that separates the great blue and white herbaceous border from the Camel garden. It is 1.8m/6ft high, made of 300mm/1ft square trellis of pressure-treated larch which is painted with Cuprinol every four years. Trained on it are roses ('Fimbriata', 'Albertine', 'Etoile de Hollande', 'Lawrence Johnston') and – an unusual sight – the blue *Campanula lactiflora* which in Scotland shoots up to 2.4m/8ft high. Narrow beds planted entirely with *Bergenia cordifolia* on one side and lavender on the other, form a solid visual base for the trellis.

Trellis fixed to walls may emphasize architectural features and provide a disciplined support for climbing plants. At TATTON PARK the 'L' borders are backed with 3.6m/12ft high brick walls punctuated by regular buttresses surmounted by ornamental urns. These urns are, in fact, chimney pots for the fires that, in the nineteenth century, were used to heat the walls (which are hollow) to protect delicate fruit blossom in spring. Old trellis has been fixed to these walls and meticulously shaped round the buttresses. At present, however, the trellis is gradually being replaced with pressure-treated wooden slate-laths painted with timber-stain to re-create its original texture.

A classical temple of 1760 at Blickling Hall was approached from the north-west by a stately avenue of lime and oak which was virtually entirely destroyed in the storm of 1987. It is now being replanted in oak.

AVENUES

The predecessor of the avenue was the broad path or ride – called an *allée* in France – cut through woodland. André Le Nôtre made these *allées* an essential part of his gardening vocabulary. To emphasize their length he would sometimes taper them. He would sometimes also extend them beyond the horizon; Humphry Repton, too, admired an avenue that 'climbs up a hill and, passing over the summit, leaves the fancy to conceive its determination.' In Britain the avenue had its heyday in the seventeenth and early eighteenth centuries as a way of asserting a great landowner's domination of the landscape and proclaiming his importance. Visually it might serve two essential purposes – as an overture to the house and as a link between garden and landscape. A grand avenue leading up to and framing the entrance of a house makes an emphatic statement and arouses in the visitor suitably receptive feelings about what lies ahead.

William Kent believed that avenues could be 'clumped', that is to say planted in groups at irregular intervals, maintaining the essential axis but also permitting views across it. There is an avenue of this sort at HINTON AMPNER where the original 1720 lime avenue has been 'clumped' but the feeling of the axis revitalized by placing a temple at the garden end and an obelisk in the field. To the landscape improvers of the later eighteenth century this smacked too much of unnatural formality and 'Capability' Brown disposed of many of them when creating his own, more natural, vistas.

By the middle of the nineteenth-century, avenues once again were widely planted and many were made with the new and fashionable conifers of the day – cedars, Monkey Puzzles and Wellingtonias. Few remain, but an attractive example survives at the remarkable BIDDULPH GRANGE in Staffordshire. Here, James Bateman, who started the garden in 1845, planted an avenue of Deodars (*Cedrus deodara*) – a then new tree introduced from the Himalaya only in 1831.

The essential structural idea of the avenue is to create a vista by repeated planting of pairs of plants of identical size at regular intervals. It can be done on a very modest scale – it is quite possible to have an avenue of potted pelargoniums. Long before the use of avenues in the landscape the idea had been used on a much more intimate scale in Renaissance Italy where a double row of pencil cypresses was a common ingredient – giving shade and structure. Within a garden, an avenue of clipped shapes – such as that of box domes making an ornamental axis linking different compartments at TINTINHULL – may both be extremely decorative and have a powerful structural effect.

Lines of great trees set in the landscape are what most of us think of as avenues. The avenue of Spanish Chestnuts (*Castanea sativa*) at CROFT CASTLE, planted in the seventeenth century, and the eighteenth-century lime (*Tilia × europaea*) avenue at DUNHAM MASSEY are outstanding examples. In recent times Dutch Elm Disease has been the occasion for much replanting, sometimes using less familiar trees. At HIDCOTE the north avenue of Huntingdon Elms has been replaced with alternate Turkey Oak

At Crathes Castle trellis is used to divide space and support climbing plants.

The avenue of limes at Saltram House, planted after 1884, is a unique example of a substantial avenue planted within a garden. It is 237m/780ft long. The trees are underplanted with Cyclamen hederifolium *and old varieties of narcissus.*

At Nymans an avenue of common lime (Tilia × europaea) curves round the south-west corner of the park. The gnarled trunks have a powerful presence in the winter. Apart from their decorative and structural roles, avenues provide valuable wind shelter.

'Puddings' of clipped yew form an emphatic avenue leading across the forecourt to the front door at Lytes Cary. Looking from the doorway, the vista is satisfyingly closed by a dovecote, echoing the yew shapes, in a field beyond the garden.

(*Quercus cerris*) and Hornbeam (*Carpinus betulus*). Re-planting of avenues on the grand scale is undertaken at National Trust gardens. Bridgeman's double avenue of elms at WIMPOLE HALL, destroyed by age and Dutch Elm Disease, has been replanted using limes. These trees were selected from specimens at Wimpole of *Tilia cordata* and *T. platyphyllos* and hybrids between them. From these a few, matching in general habit, were propagated in quantity by grafting. The trees have been carefuly mixed in the final planting to reproduce the slight random variations that would have arisen in an old avenue of trees propagated by seed. These grand replantings, exciting to see in great historic estates and such a vital ingredient of their character, is of little practical relevance to the average gardener. But the principle of the rhythmical repetition of plants of the same type and size is applicable to any garden – large or small.

At POWIS CASTLE there is a charming avenue of pyramid-shaped apple trees, with a few pear trees, in the old kitchen gardens. They were planted in about 1912 and are now 3m/10ft high. They are extremely decorative in flower and, with their good strong shapes, have a powerful structural presence, marching in stately fashion down the gentle slope. They are clipped when dormant, which both shapes them and stimulates the growth of flowering spurs and a dense structure of branches. Old trees have had to be replaced from time to time. Maiden trees are planted and side shoots are pegged down to hold them horizontal. In order to stimulate the formation of further side shoots it is essential to trim the vertical leader, removing about one-third of the year's growth during the dormant period. To keep the leader as straight as possible always choose a bud on the opposite side to that taken the previous year. As a framework of sturdy horizontal branches is formed at the bottom it can be used to tie horizontal the new growth further up the stem. The trees are planted in circles 1.5m/5ft in diameter cut into the turf. Each circle is filled with a decorative pool of shallow-rooted foliage plants underplanted with spring bulbs – the non-flowering form of *Stachys olympica* 'Silver Carpet', silver *Lamium maculatum*, either 'Beacon Silver' or 'White Nancy', Golden Marjoram (*Origanum vulgare* 'Aureum') with grape hyacinths (*Muscari armeniacum* 'Blue Spike') underplanted among the *Stachys* and Stars of Bethlehem (*Ornithogalum umbellatum*) under the marjoram.

Avenues of small ornamental trees have great structural presence within the garden. In the rose garden at SIZERGH there was, until 1983, a short avenue of limes which succumbed to Slime Flux disease. They have been replaced by an elegant rowan – *Sorbus aucuparia* 'Beissneri' – planted at intervals of 9m/30ft in rows 5.4m/18ft apart. These rowans will never grow much higher than 15m/50ft and, in this rather enclosed setting, are a happier choice than the limes that preceded them. The avenue leads from a pair of fine stone gate piers to a bench placed before a curved screen of yew. An avenue of this sort – which is only 45m/150ft long – is perfectly possible in many medium-sized gardens. In choosing trees for a small avenue within a garden, apart from the essential matter of ultimate size, it is important to think carefully about all the decorative aspects – foliage, flower, fruit, bark and habit of growth.

An avenue of topiary shapes can provide a firm axis about which other structural elements may be deployed. This is shown very well at LYTES CARY in Somerset where an avenue of clipped yew domes surmounted with shallow cones lines a paved path running down the middle of the forecourt. The atmosphere of the forecourt is calm and formal. Against one wall are mounded buttresses of box. There is a boundary of privet hedging and, on either side of the entrance gate, box hedges. Looking from the house along the path one notices that the clipped yew shapes echo the shape of a dovecote in a field that is centred on the path's axis. It makes a strikingly effective link between the formality of the garden and its rural surroundings.

TOPIARY

Topiary, or what used to be called 'vegetable sculpture', is the ornamental shaping of shrubs and trees. It goes back at least to Roman times – Pliny the Elder (AD 23-79) referred to ornamental gardening as *opus topiarium* and the gardener responsible for it as the *topiarius*. Clipped box, fashioned into all sorts of fanciful shapes, was certainly known in Pliny the Younger's time. With the revival of classical learning topiary re-emerged in Renaissance Italy where it became an absolutely essential part of the gardening vocabulary. Alberti, in *De Re Aedificatoria* (1452) describes his ideal garden, which would have topiary cut into remarkable shapes. It was possible that Alberti himself advised on the design of the garden of the Rucellai palace in Florence which had topiary made into 'spheres, porticoes, temples, vases, urns, apes, donkeys, oxen, a bear, giants, men, women, warriors, a harpy, philosophers, Popes, cardinals.' In England the fashion for topiary started in Tudor times, and there are late-fifteenth-century references to *opere topiario* at the Earl of Northumberland's castle at Wressle in Yorkshire and Henry VIII's accounts show purchases of plants for topiary at Hampton Court. By the end of the seventeenth century topiary was found even in the park at Woburn, as described by Celia Fiennes in the 1690s: 'some of the trees are kept cut in works and the shape of severall beasts.' The engravings of early-eighteenth-century gardens by Kip, almost without exception formal in character, show how extensive the use of topiary had become by that time. But by then advanced horticultural taste was already attacking topiary. Alexander Pope in an essay in *The Guardian* (1713) mocked 'myrtles tortured into

Above: Snow emphasises the permanent value of evergreen topiary at Levens Hall. Opposite: The knot garden at Westbury Court, filled with marigolds and Echium plantagineum.

At The Courts a contorted shape of clipped yew originally represented 'the dancing bears'
and is now a green riddle. Rows of Irish yews, fringed with contrasting silver wormwood, have an
attractively purposeful air.

ship shapes, poops and prows, waves billowing out of boxwood' and all the more extravagant examples of the 'Tonsure of Greens', as he called it. The landscape movement of Lancelot 'Capability' Brown in the second half of the eighteenth century swept formality aside and with it topiary. Of the great gardens there were few survivors from the classical age of the English formal garden. In J.C. Loudon's monumental *An Encyclopaedia of Gardening* (1822) there are only a few lines on topiary –

'very appropriate for parterres and other scenes in the ancient style.' In the middle of the nineteenth century there was a tremendous revival, and by the turn of the century, despite the influence of the Robinsonian 'natural' garden, it was once again a common feature. Victorian gardeners saw it as a way of giving a house a desirably venerable appearance. John D. Sedding in *Garden-Craft Old and New* (1891) breezily dismisses the misgivings of the 'natural' gardeners, 'I have no more scruple in using the scissors upon tree and shrub, where trimness is desirable, than I have in mowing the turf of the lawn that once represented a virgin world. There is a quaint charm in the results of topiary art, in the prim imagery of evergreens, that all ages have felt.'

'The prim imagery of evergreens' contributes immensely to the character of a garden. It can also, by some odd alchemy, give an air of fairly instant antiquity. Topiary seems permanent, solidly unchanging. The yews that lie below the mount at PACKWOOD, known as the Multitude, were planted in the 1840s. The mount itself is eighteenth century and the helical box-edged path nineteenth century. In the 1890s Reginald Blomfield, the connoisseur of the formal garden, was convinced that the Multitude dated back to Cromwellian times. Few of the gardens we know today whose essential character depends on topiary are much older than the nineteenth century. At Cranborne Manor virtually all the topiary, such a vital part of

Beyond the walled garden at Packwood House, the great old yews known as 'The Multitude' rise formidably above. Elegant eighteenth-century pavilions in each corner have windows overlooking the topiary.

The mount at Packwood House surrounded by the columnar yews known as 'The Apostles'. Although the layout of 'The Apostles' dates from the seventeenth century, the religious significance attached to it is a modern interpretation.

Late nineteenth-century topiary at Chirk Castle, originally in the shape of pointed 'witches' hats', has lost its clear outline but the accidental patterns of slopes and angles introduce a lively new dimension not outfaced by the castle ramparts.

the atmosphere of this early-seventeenth-century house, has been planted by the present Lady Salisbury. Another factor that quickly gives a feeling of antiquity is that it is remarkably difficult to maintain geometric shapes for long. At CHIRK CASTLE the topiary was made in the late nineteenth century. In the formal garden a long path is lined with pairs of yews clipped into cones with cylindrical bases. A photograph taken in the 1930s shows these to be crisp and precisely geometrical. Today, though, they are attractively irregular, billowing with ungovernable curves and appearing to be immensely venerable.

Apart from a few deciduous plants (for example, viburnum or willow) that can be trimmed into mop-heads, the materials used for topiary are usually ever-green. They must have the toughness to take clipping well and, in order to make smoothly modelled shapes, should have dense small-leaved foliage. In the past many plants were commonly used – yew, box, holly, juniper, Bay, Cherry Laurel, cypress and the handsome *Phillyrea angustifolia*. This last, certainly cultivated in England since the sixteenth century, is used effectively in the replanting of the late-seventeenth-century formal garden at WESTBURY COURT. This garden was made by Maynard Colchester whose detailed account books survive and record the purchase of several 'phillereys'. Today they form handsome mounds at the centre of a formal arrangement on either side of the reconstructed parterre.

In Britain today by far the commonest plants for topiary are box and yew. For detailed modelling yew is the better plant and its new growth is sufficiently pliable to train leaders to form elaborate shapes. Box is good for simple shapes such as cones, spheres and so on, but it lacks the

*Archways of clipped yew at Hidcote Manor frame
vistas and are in themselves decorative pieces
of topiary.*

resilience of yew and will not take complicated detail. It can be trained very successfully into a standard and its crown clipped into a sphere, which is often used to great effect. It is used in this way in the knot garden at MOSELEY OLD HALL and in the Cromwellian Garden at GREYS COURT.

There are two ways of making topiary shapes: either by training and clipping – gradually building up the shape – or by allowing the plant to fill a shaped framework and clipping off any growth that extends beyond the frame. The first, 'freehand', method is the more straightforward. Also, in the tradition of what Vita Sackville-West vividly describes as 'smug broody hens, bumpy doves and coy peacocks', there is much room for latitude and the occasional slip of the shears. To start a topiary piece it is best to leave a plant for two or three years to see what sort of natural shape it forms. Plants that grow naturally in an evenly bushy way will make good geometric shapes. Others may throw out leaders which can be used to build up, say, the head and tail of a bird. Bamboos can be fixed to the plant to train leaders in the desired direction. When a leader has grown long enough, clipping its end will stimulate growth along its length so that it will bush out. If you want a particular shape in a specific place, a few plants can be kept in a vacant bed and transplanted when their natural tendencies have shown themselves. From the moment shaping starts it is important to clip as tightly as possible to thicken up the framework of branches. Feeding is very important at this stage as clipping weakens the young plant and it struggles to put on new growth.

In old pieces of topiary, branches tend to flop out, sometimes as a result of a snowfall. At LEVENS HALL and at PACKWOOD HOUSE it is part of the routine upkeep to tie such branches in. At CRATHES in Aberdeenshire, where heavy snow is a normal winter occurrence, it is never allowed to lie on the ancient yew hedges and topiary. A rake with an extension handle is used to remove it every morning after a fall.

The Pool Garden at Crathes Castle has a strong rectilinear layout with monumental blocks of clipped yew framing the square pool. This pattern of formality provides discipline for the exuberant planting of red, yellow and purple.

*Topiary shapes added to the crest of a yew hedge at Nymans echo the gables of the house. An ocean of day-lilies
froths at its base. The light-hearted formality of the topiary contrasts attractively with the naturally planted
drifts of flowers.*

In the reconstruction of the ancient topiary garden at Brickwall House, a chess-board with squares of contrasting chippings has topiary chess-pieces in ordinary and golden yew. The metal frames guide the shaping of the young plants and are later removed.

A specialized form of freehand topiary is what is known as 'poodling' on the west coast of the USA. This is an adaptation of an ancient Japanese technique of shaping evergreens (pine, box or cypress are common), giving tightly clipped rounded shapes to the foliage on the branches. It is partly a decorative technique and partly a way of controlling the size of trees, which grow extremely quickly on the west coast, in limited spaces. In addition it allows an improved air circulation to the plants – as clipping does, presumably, to poodles.

The use of frames is illustrated in an interesting new topiary chess garden designed by William Mount at Brickwall in East Sussex and planted in 1981. The chess-board is made of 1.95m/6ft 6in squares of gravel of two different colours (black granite and limestone) separated by single courses of brick laid crossways on their sides. Under the gravel are sheets of heavy-grade polyester sheeting to suppress weeds. The colours of the chess pieces are distinguished by one side being planted in Common Yew (*Taxus baccata*) and the other in its golden

A clipped Portugal Laurel rises above double herbaceous borders at Crathes Castle lending decorative structure in a profusely planted area of the garden.

form (*T. b. aurea*). The pieces, incidentally, are arranged to form a chess problem – checkmate in one move. The shapes, which are highly detailed, have been made of iron 'cages' which the plants gradually fill out. Any growth protruding beyond the 'cages' is trimmed off with secateurs in the autumn. The metal frames have 300mm/ 1ft legs which are cemented into plastic tubes buried in the ground to hold them firm. In principle the framework should eventually be removed. It is hard to see how this can be done without damaging the complicated topiary shapes. These frames can be bought ready made but they are extremely expensive.

Simple frames for geometric shapes may be valuable in a formal scheme in which regularity of size is important. But in time all topiary must get bigger, it will outgrow its frame and irregularity will creep in. For the yew obelisks that are such an important part of the parterres at CLIVEDEN and at PITMEDDEN, for example, a movable wooden frame which fits over the topiary pieces is used for the annual clipping to ensure complete uniformity of size and shape.

A rather different kind of frame is used for American frame topiary. Here, quite complicated wire frames (often in the shape of animals) have some suitable twining or climbing plant trained about them and gently shaped where necessary. Ornamental forms of ivy (*Hedera helix*) and the half-hardy small-leaved *Ficus pumila* are commonly used ingredients.

Other trees and shrubs may be given an air of formality by being clipped to form ornamental crowns. The Portugal Laurel (*Prunus lusitanica*) with its dark glossy leaves is an exceptionally attractive evergreen which lends itself well to shaping. At ERDDIG pairs of them, clipped into mop-heads, have been planted down the central vista leading away from the house. They appear to be planted in white Versailles boxes, which turn out to be sham – the boxes have no bottoms and the trees are planted in the ground. They look, from a distance, remarkably like citrus plants. Interestingly enough, William Temple in his essay 'Upon the Gardens of Epicurus' (1685) writes of 'the border set with standard laurels . . . which have the beauty of orange trees'.

At HIDCOTE the narrow-leaved form, *Prunus lusitanica* 'Myrtifolia', which also has a more compact habit of growth, makes handsome umbrella shapes that have replaced the original planting in the rose garden of clipped bays (*Laurus nobilis*), which proved insufficiently hardy in the Cotswolds. All sorts of other plants may be loosely shaped, but in many cases the resultant denaturing of the plant brings little benefit.

A formal pattern of sweeping yew hedges makes the backdrop of 'The Stage' at Bodnant. The curvaceous bench, from a design by William Kent, is raised on a dais and painted a dramatic green – giving an appropriately theatrical atmosphere.

Simple topiary blocks on a grand scale are one of the most effective garden devices. John Evelyn referred to topiary as 'hortulan architecture'. Clipped blocks of yew have a monumental presence that no other plant gives. At BODNANT they are used with dramatic simplicity in the 'theatre' at the north end of the Canal Terrace. Curved steps lead up to the 'stage' where progressively wider 'flies' of yew jut out on either side. At the back of the stage is a curved backdrop of yew with a central gap through which is visible the gnarled trunk of an old Monterey Pine (*Pinus radiata*). In front of the gap a single handsome bench copied from a William Kent design is raised on a shallow dais flanked by statues. From the bench, one looks down on to the long canal in which is reflected the charming old pin mill and to the north views of Conwy mountain. The unforced simplicity of this arrangement, and the effective use made of the tree behind it (making a connection with the woodland beyond), make this an instructive example of high drama achieved without fuss. Above all it illustrates a principle which owners of small gardens can profit from, that is, creating maximum impact with the simplest of means. In a small garden the impression of greater length can therefore be given by planting a pair of curved 'flies' near the end of the garden

BODNANT
'The Stage'

Bench

N
↑

Yew

Grass

DIMENSIONS: 12.5m × 27m (42ft × 90ft)

with a small ornamental tree behind glimpsed in the gap between them.

At BIDDULPH GRANGE the Egyptian Court is a heroic composition of massive blocks of yew with appropriately pyramidal tops flanking a grandiose stone entrance guarded by two pairs of huge stone sphinxes. This juxtaposition of monumental but harmonious shapes in quite different materials brings out the distinctive virtues of each. Its position – near the house – also makes a thematic link between plants and architecture.

Clipped Irish Yews (*Taxus baccata* 'Fastigiata') also have a powerful architectural quality. The sunken east lawn at MONTACUTE has on three sides rows of sentinel Irish Yews planted in the 1850s and now 4.5m/15ft high. These are backed by rows of the thorn *Crataegus* × *lavallei* Carrierei' which naturally form well-rounded crowns. Both in shape and in colour (the young leaf is an elegant downy grey) they make an effective foil to the dark, fastigiate yews. In the centre of the lawn is a fine pool and fountain. The effect is both restrained and dramatic.

The Egyptian Court in the great nineteenth-century garden at Biddulph Grange shows a carefully worked-out harmony of massive topiary shapes and monumental sculptures. Two pairs of sphinxes guard the great portal of yew.

Spheres of clipped box play an architectural role and emphasise a gate leading from the courtyard to the rose garden at Sissinghurst Castle. In richly planted gardens, simple topiary of this sort has emphatic presence.

At Nymans large topiary animals are set in gravel. This crested duck, made of clipped box, has had a dead leaf added by the gardener as an eye. Humorous formality of this sort has an agreeably deflationary effect.

Topiary as a contrast, giving ornamental structure to an informal area, can be extremely effective. The Wall Garden at NYMANS has an outstanding collection of ornamental trees and shrubs in the informal setting of an old orchard. At the centre, herbaceous borders (which William Robinson helped to plan for the Countess of Rosse's aunt) meet at an Italian fountain of pale-pink marble. Surrounding the fountain are four yew drums surmounted by elaborate topiary crowns, 3.6m/12ft high overall. The framework for

the crowns was originally formed with a wire armature which is still in place but now superseded by beautifully trained and grafted yew branches. This decorative topiary introduces a lively structural presence at the heart of an otherwise informal scheme.

Humorous topiary is exceedingly difficult to handle well. One has to be a master gardener to get away with something as whimsical as the fox eternally chased by hounds that embellishes one of the yew hedges at grow upwards and has been clipped into a lollipop shape. It provides a series of punctuation marks which make a lively decoration.

A similar effect has been achieved at WESTBURY COURT. Here, a remarkable late seventeenth-century Dutch-style canal-garden has been carefully restored from the Kip engraving of 1707 which served as the basis for the restoration which began in 1971. Facing an elegant brick garden pavilion a slender canal has, on either side, yew hedges 1.2m/4ft high. Every seventh yew has been allowed to grow above the top of the hedge and has been shaped into a lollipop. Equidistant between each lollipop there is a tightly clipped cone of Common Holly. These ornaments, thoroughly in keeping with the formal mood, provide an effective contrast to the austere simplicity of the hedges and mirror-like canals.

Hedges can be shaped to provide an architectural counterpoint to buildings. The tops of hedges at NYMANS have been clipped into tall, pyramid crenellations, complete with structural 'shoulders', that echo the gaunt gables of the burnt-out south wing of the house. At PIDMEDDEN giant yew buttresses seem to support the retaining wall of the formal garden and flare out where they meet the wall. The buttresses are ornamented with pine-cone-shaped finials and their tops are clipped into slopes that repeat the ogival curves of the pavilions at each end of the wall.

At PACKWOOD, in the walled garden, 'stalls' of shaped hedging make ornamental enclosures for a planting of roses. Each stall is 2.7m/9ft square backed by a 3m/10ft high brick wall. The sides of the stalls are made of yew sloping from a height of 1.5m/5ft down to 450mm/18in and the fronts are made of dwarf box 300mm/1ft high. Each stall is filled with plants of a single Floribunda rose, alternate stalls planted with red ('Lilli Marlene') and yellow ('Bright Smiles'). On the wall behind each stall there is climbing rose of the other colour, the creamy yellow 'Leverkusen' and deep red 'Dortmund'.

A sprightly topiary fox is eternally chased by a pack of hounds along the top of a yew hedge at Knightshayes Court.

KNIGHTSHAYES COURT. This tradition has, however, a long history. William Lawson in his *The Country Housewife's Garden* (1618) writes, 'Your gardener can frame your leser wood to the shape of men armed in the field, ready to give battel; of swift running greyhounds or of well scented and true running hounds to chase the deer, or hunt the Hare. This kind of hunting shall not waste your corn, nor much your coin.' The various plump birds and animals of clipped box at Nymans will elicit a grin from all but the sternest garden visitor, but I find them unhappily reminiscent of the fat ladies of saucy seaside postcards. They cause a chuckle but scarcely lift the heart.

Topiary can be combined with hedges with telling ornamental effect. At LYTES CARY a long yew hedge has at regular intervals buttresses with curved tops. At the intersection of each buttress a shoot has been allowed to

In the walled garden at Packwood House clipped 'stalls' with yew sides and box fronts have
alternate blocks of red and yellow roses. The formal compartments provide decorative structure when the
roses are not flowering.

KNOTS, MAZES AND PARTERRES

Knots and mazes are very close in spirit and in their use in the garden. Indeed, in early garden writings the two are frequently mentioned in the same context and sometimes it is hard to make a clear distinction between them. According to John Harvey in his book *Mediaeval Gardens*, 'a knot in a garden, called a mase' (maze) was a commonplace in English gardens by 1494. The parterre is essentially a sophisticated version of the knot.

KNOTS

Knots are beds in which regular patterns of some low-growing clipped plant form a decorative framework. The word comes from the resemblance to an interweaving of threads. As a decorative device it was widely used in the Middle Ages, and illuminated manuscripts often have marginal ornamentation of this kind. By the end of the sixteenth century it was a commonplace in England, much seen in the rather overwrought 'strapwork' of Jacobean plasterwork. In gardens the knot probably has its origins in the ornamental 'herbers' which in the royal houses of the late Middle Ages were deliberately sited under bedroom windows. There is a lively description from Grose's *Antiquarian Repertory* of the garden at the Palace of Richmond as it was set up for the visit of Catherine of Aragon in 1501, 'under the King's window, Queen's, and other estates, with royal knots alleyed and herbed; many marvellous beasts, as lions, dragons, and such other of

At Mount Stewart the Italian garden has parterres edged with plum-coloured Berberis thunbergii *'Atropurpurea Nana' and a golden-leaved cultivar of* Thuja occidentalis.

divers kinds, properly fashioned and carved in the ground, right well sanded.' By the seventeenth century the knot had been replaced in grander gardens by the newfangled *parterre de broderie* of which it is clearly a simple ancestor. Gervase Markham in his *The English Husbandman* (1613) says that the knot is 'of most use among the vulgar though least respected with great ones, who for the most part are wholly given over to novelties.'

There were essentially two types of knot – open and closed. The open knot consisted of a framework of low hedging (rosemary, lavender, germander, hyssop and thyme were frequently used) which left spaces which were filled with coloured gravel or sand. The colours corresponded with heraldic symbolism. In the closed knot the intervening spaces were filled with flowering plants. Fortunately, although no description survives from the heyday of knots, they continued in use long after more fashionable gardens had adopted the parterre and many later descriptions survive.

A plan dated 1671 enabled the National Trust in 1976 to reconstruct an appropriate 'closed' knot on the east side of the seventeenth-century HAM HOUSE on the exact site of the original. This is a symmetrical arrangement outlining triangles and lozenges in small-leaved box (*Buxus sempervirens* 'Suffruticosa') 220mm/9in high. These hedges are punctuated by cones in Common Box (*Buxus sempervirens*) 900mm/3ft high. Gravel paths edged with planks run between the beds. The beds are filled with either Dwarf Cotton Lavender (*Santolina chamaecyparissus nana*) or Dutch Lavender. Both these are clipped in the spring, usually in mid-April and fed with a slow-release organic

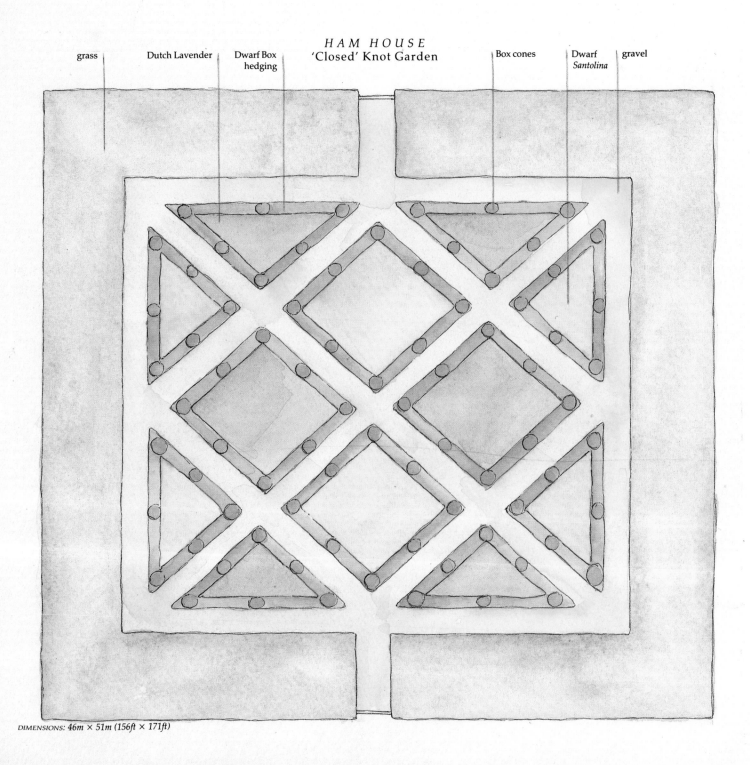

HAM HOUSE
'Closed' Knot Garden

grass Dutch Lavender Dwarf Box hedging Box cones Dwarf *Santolina* gravel

DIMENSIONS: 46m × 51m (156ft × 171ft)

The knot at Ham House was reconstructed from a plan dated 1671 and has been placed on the original site, overlooked by the east windows of the house. Blocks of a single plant fill each compartment and the design is emphasised by the contrasting gravel.

The knot garden at Little Moreton Hall was reconstructed from an Elizabethan design – a formal design appropriate to the house.

fertilizer. Neither of these plants is long-lived, and the foliage colour is much better in young plants: they are therefore entirely replaced every four years for the *Santolina* and every five for the lavender.

This knot depends for its effect on the contrast of the leaf-colour of its ingredients and the rhythmic formality of hedges, paths and clipped shapes. Views of it are carefully framed by the window cut in the yew hedge which runs along a raised bank to the south or from the tunnels of mixed hornbeam and yew on either side. The whole arrangement is directly overlooked by the windows of the house.

An 'open' knot, copied from Leonard Meager's *The English Gardener*, has been laid out at the Tudor house LITTLE MORETON HALL. Although Meager's book was published in 1670, this design probably dates back to the Elizabethan period. Dwarf-box hedges 220mm/9in high

outline beds filled with gravel that form an intricate pattern.

The box used here seems to be rather a mixed bag, varying much in colour and leaf-size neither of which detracts from its charm. At each corner of the open knot, an obelisk of yew has been trimmed to exactly the same height (2.1m/7ft) as the enclosing yew hedges. On two sides the formality, although continued, is done so in a very decorative scheme. A 1.8m/6ft wide bed contains rows of standard gooseberries 1.2m/4ft high, each planted in a clipped square of some herbaceous plant known to have been available in Tudor times – Wall Germander (*Teucrium chamaedrys*), strawberries, Woodruff (*Galium odoratum*), London Pride (*Saxifraga × urbium*) and so on.

The setting of a knot may contribute enormously to its effectiveness. At MOSELEY OLD HALL, a small seventeenth-

LITTLE MORETON HALL
'Open' Knot Garden

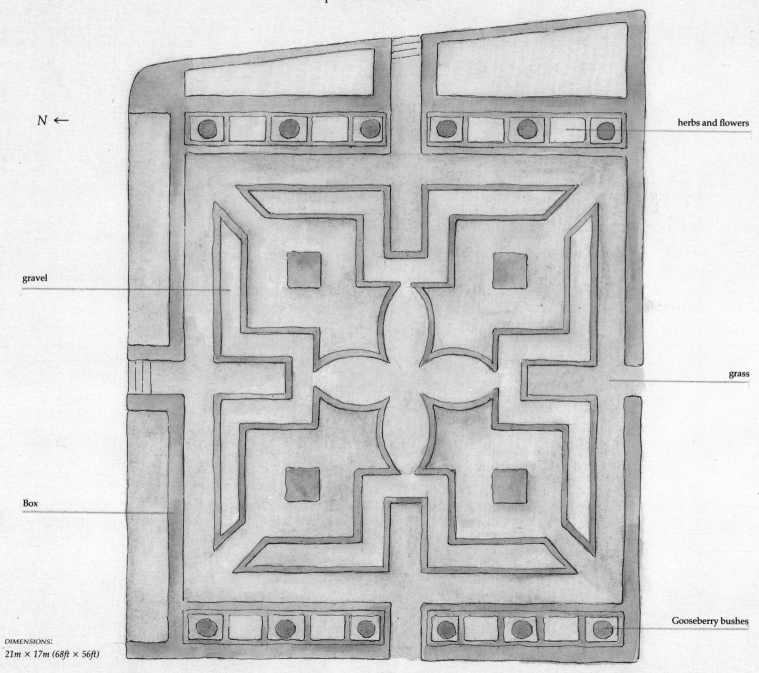

N ←

herbs and flowers

gravel

grass

Box

Gooseberry bushes

DIMENSIONS:
21m × 17m (68ft × 56ft)

MOSELEY OLD HALL
Knot Garden

Box hedging

Standard Box

gravel

N

DIMENSIONS: *21m × 13m (69ft × 42ft)*

Knots and parterres were designed to be seen from above – either from a window or a raised terrace. At Moseley Old Hall the reconstructed knot, copied from a mid-seventeenth-century design, gives a convincing impression of a formal garden of the time.

century house, there is a knot which seems exceptionally successful in this way. The knot itself is copied from a design of 1640 made by the Reverend Walter Stonehouse. A series of scalloped and circular beds edged with dwarf box is interlaced with gravel paths. In the centre of each circular bed is a standard box with a spherical crown. Materials have been carefully chosen: the paths are made of sandy gravel; the scalloped beds have small pebbles; and the circular beds have much larger pebbles. The gravel and pebbles are laid on polystyrene sheeting which runs close to the box edging. On one side is a beautifully made tunnel of arcaded 'carpenter's work' copied from an illustration in Thomas Hill's *A Gardener's Labyrinth* (1577). It is richly festooned with the purple-leaved grapevine *Vitis vinifera* 'Purpurea', the Virgin's Bower Clematis (*Clematis flammula*) and another clematis, *C. viticella*, whose purple flowers intermingle harmoniously with the leaves of the vine.

At their feet are bushes of Old English Lavender, aquilegias and *Geranium versicolor*. This tunnel leads into a shady hazel-nut walk which joins a narrow paved path flanked by pairs of quinces, medlars and mulberries down the other side of the knot. The whole lies immediately below the windows of the house.

MAZES

The principle of the maze or labyrinth is of great antiquity. Herodotus, writing in the fourth century BC, describes in great detail an Egyptian labyrinth that was already immensely old. There is also the maze that Daedalus made on Minos to conceal the Minotaur – the archetypal labyrinthine legend. In England the earliest maze is engraved on rock in Cornwall and dates from 1800-1400 BC. In Christian philosophy the maze had a special meaning as a symbol of the soul in pursuit of the elusive goal of perfection, and in the Middle Ages became a widespread decorative motif. As a garden feature the maze seems to have its origins, like so many other formal garden devices, in the Italian Renaissance. Four mazes are shown in a 1573 engraving of the Villa d'Este. These seem to be hedge mazes rather than the two-dimensional patterns usually found in the earlier period. A book published in Antwerp in 1583, de Vries's *Hortorum Viridariorumque Formae*, shows several designs for mazes of great complexity. Whether or not they were actually built does not matter. The idea was clearly firmly in the horticultural consciousness of the late sixteenth century.

The Archbishop's maze at Greys Court. It is full of religious symbolism relating to the soul's quest for perfection.

The great yew hedge maze at Hampton Court, originally planted in 1690 for William of Orange, seems to have been the first garden hedge maze in England. It is planted in yew, 2.1m/7ft high. Most early mazes were 'unicursal' – that is to say, there was only one route. The Hampton Court maze, however, is full of deceptions and puzzles. It has been the model for mazes all over the world.

In the first half of the eighteenth century mazes continued to be built, but they were another victim of landscaping. In the nineteenth century mazes again became fashionable. W. A. Nesfield designed several, including that at Shrubland Park which still survives.

There is a renaissance of interest in mazes today and several have been made in recent years. At GREYS COURT the Archbishop's Maze, designed in 1981 by Adrian Fisher and Randoll Coate, was inspired by a reference to solving 'the secret of the maze of life' in an address by the Archbishop of Canterbury, Dr Robert Runcie. This is not a puzzle maze but one in which the tracing of the route has symbolic meaning. It is made of turf with narrow brick paths (only three bricks wide) emphasizing the loneliness of the spiritual quest. The overall layout is in the shape of a crown of thorns and the details are full of symbolism. At the centre are two crosses – the Roman and the Byzantine cross intermingle to convey the message of ecumenism. As a self-contained decorative feature it has charm and originality but it is set to one side of the garden, overlooking countryside, and not structurally linked to the rest of the garden. At Leeds Castle the same designers completed in 1988 a spectacular puzzle maze of yew whose goal is the entrance to a magnificent new grotto linked to underground passages by which one emerges from the maze. This maze too is full of symbolism. Leeds was the site of the castle inhabited by the devout Queen Eleanour, wife of Edward I. The maze traces the shape of a chalice with the mound as the host, in memory of the daily masses sung in the castle chapel after Eleanour's death in 1290.

The sprawling and monumental maze of cherry laurel (Prunus laurocerasus) at Glendurgan was made in 1833 by Alfred Fox on a steep slope in the valley of the River Helford. Its asymmetrical shape well suits the woodland garden that surrounds it.

A COLOUR MAZE

coloured brick

Box hedging

DIMENSIONS: 9m × 9m (30ft × 30ft)

A problem with the maintenance of hedge mazes is that in time the walls encroach on each other, the passage becomes too narrow and increasing deprivation of light will cause die-back at the base. At TATTON PARK there is a nineteenth-century copy of the trapezoidal Hampton Court maze – but planted in beech. The hedges are 2.4m/8ft high and the paths have become so narrow that die-back has made the lower parts of the hedges so full of gaps as to be practically transparent. As an experiment a section of the hedge has been cut back to the trunks and has been lined to its full height with heavy-gauge plastic-coated wire netting. This both prevents over-eager visitors taking short cuts and will provide a firm guide for future clipping.

The Minotaur Colour Maze has been specially designed by Adrian Fisher for readers of this book. Mazes are usually associated with gardening on a grand scale. This maze has been designed to provide a challenging puzzle in a modest area. Designed on a 450mm/18in module, the maze is 9m/30ft × 9m/30ft. This can be reduced to a 300mm/12in module (making a maze 6m/20ft × 6m/20ft) or increased to 600mm/2ft (making 12m/40ft × 12m/40ft).

The puzzle of this maze is made more complex by the coloured paths. Brick, cream, light buff and red paving slabs could be used with dark brown in the centre. The rule is to change the colour of your path every time you reach a junction square. The goal is the central square.

In this design the paths are bordered by low strips of hedging of the same width. An appropriate hedge could be made of the shrubby honeysuckle *Lonicera nitida* 'Ernest Wilson' which has exceptionally small leaves. *Lonicera pileata*, with small bright green leaves, is another possibility. The only problem with *Lonicera* is that it needs frequent clipping, and the more slow growing Box (*Buxus sempervirens*) may be preferred. This could be planted in different colour forms, for example, gold and silver variegated. The hedges should be trimmed 450mm/ 18in high.

PARTERRES

Parterres are level beds divided into some regular and usually symmetrical pattern. The word parterre suggests that this is a feature especially associated with French gardens – and so it is. But in one form or another it is of much more ancient origin. The great Muslim gardens of southern Spain – influenced by the classical Persian gardens, with their divison of flat areas into symmetrical geometric shapes with a central fountain or canal – are remarkably similar to the enclosed parterres of Renaissance France. These Muslim gardens also very often had sunken beds with flowers growing to the level of the surrounding area, like colourful eastern rugs. In Renaissance France the great maker of parterres was Claude Mollet, the royal gardener in the sixteenth century. By the seventeenth century the different types of parterres had become firmly codified. The 'embroidered' parterre (*parterre de broderie*) consisted of swirling arabesques of low clipped hedging, very often with plain or coloured gravel or sand spread between the shapes. The usual material for these has been the small-leaved box (*Buxus sempervirens* 'Suffruticosa') which was introduced in the sixteenth century, but for the very earliest examples, as Claude Mollet put it, 'very few people of rank wanted box in their gardens' and more exotic plants of different shades of green were used. These, however, needed frequent and costly replacing and Mollet found that his grand clients began to understand the charms of long-lived box. The other standard form was the cut-turf parterre (*parterre à l'anglaise*) in which decorative shapes were made by cutting out sections of turf.

The French-style parterre made an early appearance in England where in the grander gardens it swiftly replaced the knot. Claude Mollet's son André came to England and designed gardens both at St James's Palace for Charles I and at Wimbledon for Henrietta Maria. Illustrations survive of Wimbledon showing parterres with bold swirling patterns. After the Restoration the parterre

At Westbury Court accurate restoration of the garden was possible because of detailed accounts and a Kip engraving of 1717. It was not possible to reconstruct this knot in exactly the same place but the design is identical to the original.

The Fuchsia Garden at Hidcote Manor is a box-edged parterre with two seasonal displays. In spring there are carpets of Scilla siberica 'Spring Beauty'. These are followed in early summer by three different forms of fuchsia which flower until late autumn.

remained immensely fashionable, as many of Kip's early-eighteenth-century engravings show. Like many formal garden devices it all but disappeared in the later eighteenth century. However, there was a tremendous revival in the Victorian period and parterres of great complexity were made, many of which survive – for example those at TATTON PARK and WADDESDON MANOR. In the middle of the nineteenth century they were particularly associated with the craze for bedding plants in which garden owners vied with each other in extravagant ostentation. But underlying the craze there were important experiments on the effects of juxtaposing blocks and ribbons of colour. In the twentieth century, rather than a distinctive modern style emerging, new parterres tend towards historical authenticity.

It became a general rule in France that the more elaborate parterres should be close to the house – partly because of their association with the architectural complexities of the house and partly because their decorative character could best be appreciated viewed from the windows. This principle applies today at both Versailles and Vaux-le-Vicomte. When parterres lie some little distance from the house there is invariably a raised walk from which they may be viewed – as at Chenonceaux. In Britain the same principle was observed.

The 'great garden' at PITMEDDEN in Aberdeenshire is an ambitious and beautifully executed recreation of seventeenth-century Scottish parterres. The original house was burnt down but handsome garden walls, pavilions, gate piers and double staircase survive. The parterres lie at some distance from the site of the house across a wide terrace from which one looks down on to the high-walled garden. It is divided into four parterres, three of which are based on seventeenth-century plans for the garden at Holyroodhouse; the fourth shows the arms of the Seton family whose seat Pitmedden was. Down the centre runs an avenue of clipped yew obelisks. The outlines of the parterres are traced in hedges of box 450mm/18in high

and planted up with an elaborate scheme of summer annuals. This is no doubt historically incorrect but, nonetheless, extremely effective. Sixty thousand annuals are raised every year on the premises and bedded out between mid-May and mid-June. Colour schemes vary from year to year, except for the coat of arms whose colours have heraldic meaning. Plants are chosen as far as possible so they do not grow very much higher than the surrounding hedge. There is an elaborate programme of maintenance which keeps the parterres in impeccable condition. In midwinter the beds are dug over and enriched with mushroom compost. At the end of March or the beginning of April the box is clipped. This may seem much too early – running the risk of frost damage – but it must be completed, and it takes a long time, before the bedding out starts. All the intricate detail is clipped by hand, the remainder with electric clippers. All this is done by eye, although every four years clipping is done against a horizontal line to maintain an even height over the whole parterre. In early May Vitax Q4 is raked in before

The north-east parterre at Pitmedden with an earlier planting of petunias. Experiments are made with different combinations of bedding plants.

PITMEDDEN
North-East Parterre

Based on a 17th-century design for the gardens of Holyroodhouse, this parterre uses modern bedding schemes to great effect. Here, apart from the permanent planting of grass and box hedging (a special form of Buxus sempervirens unique to Pitmedden), the planting is of two contrasting marigolds – the golden yellow 'Yellow Boy' and the orange-yellow 'Boy O'Boy'. About 9,500 plants are needed for this area which is 30 × 40 m/33 × 44 yds. Five tons of farmyard manure is dug into the beds in winter and 50 kilos of Vitax Q4 raked in just before the summer plants are put in in the late spring. The box hedges are clipped once a year in spring before the bedding out. Grass is mown, and edges trimmed, weekly. The gravel is hoed weekly and both gravel and soil are topped up every five years. To suppress the germination of weed seeds Simazine is sprayed onto the gravel every other year in early spring.

N →

Marigold 'Boy O'Boy'   Marigold 'Yellow Boy'

Box

gravel

DIMENSIONS: 30m × 40m 33 × 44 yds.

An Edwardian parterre at Erddig has been meticulously recreated with spring and summer plantings chosen carefully to fit the architectural setting. In spring two different colours of tulip harmonise with the old brick walls. Mounds of clipped box give permanent structure.

bedding starts. In this northerly part of Britain the longer summer and autumn days stimulate vigorous flowering – which may continue in undiminished flow until the end of September. In October-November the dead growth is removed and the cycle of maintenance starts once again.

The Edwardian parterres at ERDDIG on the east front are overlooked by the windows of the saloon. On the other side are ornamental walls with Dutch gables made to look like the façades of pavilions. The parterres were laid out in 1905 and their Edwardian character has been carefully preserved. They lie on either side of the path that leads away from the steps down from the saloon. They are perfectly symmetrical, built up of a pattern of L-shaped and square beds, domes of clipped box and a central fountain with a moulded-stone surround. The planting is changed twice a year for spring and summer. It is never exactly the same from year to year. In the spring of 1988 the planting consisted of lily-flowered tulips planted among forget-me-nots; the pale pink 'China Pink' with white forget-me-nots and the deeper red 'Red Shine' with pink. These beds are edged with a fringe of the decorative grass *Festuca glauca* which is divided annually to keep it dense. There are also square beds edged with the almost black strap-like leaves of *Ophiopogon planiscapus nigrescens* surrounding a flat cushion of silver-grey *Santolina chamaecyparissus nana*. On either side, under the 'pavilion' walls, narrow box-edged beds are filled with the tall lily-flowered tulip 'White Triumphator' underplanted with blue forget-me-not. This lively yet formal scheme, with the pink and red tulips echoing the colour of the old brick of the house, makes a harmonious juncture between the house and the more austere formal garden beyond, with its axial canal and pleached alleys. The summer bedding scheme in 1988, in colours of pink, blue and purple, was planted with lilac impatiens, pale pink pelargonium, purple *Verbena rigida*, standard trained *Plumbago auriculata* (formerly *P. capensis*) and the antirrhinum 'Lavender Lady'. A simplified version of parterres of this sort, with labour-reducing permanent planting and with bulbs and bedding plants, could be adapted for quite small gardens.

A Victorian parterre of special interest is the one at Oxburgh Hall planted in about 1845 by Sir Henry Paston-Bedingfield. It is taken from a design for *parterres de broderie* from John James's *Theory and Practice of Gardening* (1712 – a translation of d'Argenville's *La Théorie et la Pratique du Jardinage*). The compartments are outlined in box and some are filled with permanent plantings of *Santolina chamaecyparissus nana* and *Ruta graveolens* 'Jackman's Blue'. Summer bedding includes ageratums, French marigolds and the pelargonium 'Paul Crampel'.

Some connection with the architectural surroundings, whether in colour or form, gives a parterre a sense of harmony and purpose. The small parterre at MOTTISFONT ABBEY, designed by Norah Lindsay between the wars, follows in dwarf box the pattern of the fanlight to the garden door behind it. The cruciform paths are lined with dwarf lavender. Seasonal plantings vary but a typical arrangement might be spring plantings of the pale yellow Darwin tulip 'Niphetos' underplanted with forget-me-nots followed by summer bedding of cherry pie (*Heliotropium* × *hybridum*), deep red antirrhinums and violet *Verbena* × *hybrida*.

Simple parterres, with a quite restricted range of plants, can be very effective. At HIDCOTE the Fuchsia Garden achieves a charming and long-lasting effect with simplicity. It consists of two identical parterres lying on either side of a brick path. Each parterre has an oval shape surrounded by quadrants cut round the oval. In their simplicity they are more in the tradition of the 'closed' knot. They are outlined in 200mm/8in high hedges of small-leaved box (*Buxus sempervirens* 'Suffruticosa'). In early spring the beds are dazzling with the intensely blue flowers of the Siberian Squill (*Scilla siberica*). This bulb is very easy to satisfy and will seed itself obligingly. The scillas are followed by hardy fuchsias – in the oval beds

The parterres at Cliveden, which now correspond much more closely in spirit to the original eighteenth-century design.

Fuchsia magellanica 'Variegata' with cream-margined leaves and in each of the quadrant beds either the much smaller *F.* 'Tom Thumb' (nearer the central path) or *F.* 'Lady Thumb' (at the back).

Flowers are by no means essential for a successful parterre. At CLIVEDEN the parterres that lie below the great south terrace of the house are composed of broad strips of interlocking triangles outlined in ordinary box punctuated at the corners by cones of yew. Plans for these parterres were made in 1713 by André Le Nôtre's nephew Claude Desgots, but never executed. In the mid-nineteenth century the idea was revived by the head gardener John Fleming who carried out an immensely complicated scheme of beds edged in spruce and privet and filled with rhododendrons and azaleas. Spring and summer bedding plants in prodigal quantities were wheeled in and out: in spring alone 20,000 plants and 10,000 tulips. William Robinson went to see it in 1872 and pronounced it 'one of the most repulsive examples of the extra formal school, (thrusting) itself in a rather awkward manner into the grand landscape.' The arrangement today uses blocks of grey-leaved plants – *Senecio* 'Sunshine' and *Santolina chamaecyparissus* in alternate beds. These are clipped hard back in June, fed and liberally watered. Later in the year the plants are clipped over again to make sure no flowers appear. It is a grand arrangement, appropriate to the restrained, Italianate character of this part of the garden. Another Italian ingredient is the magnificent balustrade edging the terrace which Lord Astor bought from the Villa Borghese in Rome and set up in 1896. In the huge expanse of the parterre the only colours are the different greens of the box hedging, the grass of the lawn, the deep green of the yew cones and the two shades of grey. Cuttings of the *Senecio* and the *Santolina* are kept to replace plants that die. Mr Philip Cotton, the Head Gardener, finds that dense plantings of this sort tend to retain moisture at the roots which makes them especially vulnerable to frost.

TATTON PARK
Parterre (Summer Planting)

Chamaecyparis pisifera 'Squarrosa'

Dahlia 'Princess Marie José'

Juniperus communis 'Hibernica'

Box

Ageratum 'Blue Mink'

Armeria maritima hedge

white chippings

grass

Here, in the Italian Garden, a pair of grand parterres, designed originally by Sir Joseph Paxton in 1863 when he was Head Gardener near by at Chatsworth, has been restored on a grand scale using early photographs. The beds are separated by continuous strips of 6 mm/¼ in mild steel 100 mm/4 in wide precisely shaped to fit the beds. They are anchored in the ground by 300 mm/1 ft legs at 600 mm/2 ft intervals. They are quite invisible, lying 6 mm/¼ in below the surface. They keep lawn edging impeccably sharp and absolutely prevent plants from creeping from one bed to another. This was not as expensive as it sounds and probably in the long term, from the point of view of reduced maintenance, cost-effective in a very large public garden. In small gardens a similar system on a modest scale is perfectly possible.

→ *N*

DIMENSIONS: *13.7m × 3.7m (45ft × 12ft)*

A twentieth-century box parterre at Mottisfont Abbey reflects the pattern of the fanlight in the garden door. Each summer the compartments are filled with different planting schemes. Here are red snapdragons, violet verbena and purple cherry pie.

A problem with the more elaborate knot gardens and parterres is to keep the various ingredients from inter-mingling. In the knot at WESTBURY COURT it has been found impossible to prevent coarse grass from growing through into the dwarf box, and, to solve the problem, 150mm/6in wide strips of plastic have now been buried to keep it at bay.

The principle of the parterre, more freely interpreted, can also provide a firm framework for much more varied and informal planting. At GREYS COURT a small area has been made into a charming parterre known as the Cromwellian Garden. It is divided into four beds with a cruciform arrangement of brick-and-cobble paths. Each bed is edged with box and has near its outer corner a 1.8m/6ft high standard box whose crown has been clipped into a dome. Tulips and Snake's Head Fritillaries are followed in the summer by waves of irises, purple perennial wallflower, *Santolina* and quantities of variegated London Pride (*Saxifraga* × *urbium* 'Variegata'). Forming a fourth 'wall' are laburnums espaliered on either side of the entrance. Trained on the walls are *Ceanothus* and the Moroccan Broom *Cytisus battandieri*. The whole area is only 13.8 × 18m/46 × 60ft, and its design could form the charming basis for a small town garden.

The Cromwellian garden at Greys Court is an example of patterned structure used effectively in a small space. Symmetry is emphasised by the spheres and edging of clipped box softened by clouds of London pride and other herbaceous planting.

DIRECTORY OF PLANTS

Note: where no planting distance is given, the plant shown is not considered suitable for hedging.

ACER

A. campestre, the native British Field Maple, has attractive five-lobed leaves, pink when first opening, turning to a fresh green and, in autumn, a spectacular yellow. It will grow vigorously to make a loose-textured informal hedge up to 6m/20ft. Plant: late autumn/winter. Planting distance: 450mm/18in. Clip: shape loosely in summer.

BERBERIS

B. vulgaris, the British native barberry, makes an exceptionally handsome hedge. It is deciduous, vigorous and thorny. Best as a perimeter hedge or in a wilder part of the garden. It will grow quickly to at least 2.4m/8ft high. Plant: late autumn/ winter. Planting distance: 1m/3ft. Clip: late summer, but only lightly to leave decorative berries and enough current year's growth to allow flowering (very decorative yellow racemes) the following spring.

 B. darwinii from Chile is an evergreen with very dark green leaves and outstandingly decorative turquoise berries. At TINTINHULL they are spectacular in July. It will make a very substantial hedge up to 3m/10ft high. Plant: autumn or early spring. Planting distance: 600mm/2ft. Clip: after flowering in April or May, but only loosely to leave some flowers to form berries.

 B. thunbergii from Japan is deciduous and very prickly with mid-green foliage, decorative pale-yellow flowers in the spring and bright red egg-shaped berries in the autumn. It has exceptionally brilliant red autumn foliage. *B. t. atropurpurea* has rich purple leaves. Plant: late

autumn/winter. Planting distance: 600mm/2ft. Clip: winter. There is a valuable dwarf cultivar *B. t.* '**Atropurpurea Nana**' useful for parterres and hedging.

 B. × stenophylla is evergreen with deep green foliage and handsome golden flowers in spring produced on previous year's growth. Decorative purple berries in autumn. Plant: autumn or early spring. Planting distance: 600mm/2ft. Clip: immediately after flowering in spring.

BUXUS

B. sempervirens, box, is evergreen, small-leaved, forming a compact hedge of a good fresh green. The most versatile of plants for low hedges of 600mm-1.2m/2-4ft to edge paths and borders. It is capable of forming a much taller hedge (3m/10ft or more) but is, alas, rarely seen grown in this way. At POWIS CASTLE there is an exceptional example that is over 5.4m/18ft high. The aromatic smell of its foliage in the sunshine is one of the most attractive of garden scents. It is slow-growing, tough and very long-lived – but old hedges are difficult to regenerate. It is a valuable plant for topiary. It may be shaped into geometric forms or trained effectively into a round-headed standard. Plant: September or spring. Planting distance: 300mm/1ft. Clip: once, summer/late summer.

 B. s. '**Suffruticosa**', the much smaller dwarf-leaved form of box, shares most of the characteristics of the type. It comes into its own for low edging (up to 450mm/18ft) and in knot gardens and parterres. It should be planted rather more closely – 100-150cm/4-6in.

 For vertical punctuation marks, *B. s.* '**Handsworthensis**' is an especially vigorous form that has a much larger leaf with a pronounced blue cast to the leaf colour.

CARPINUS

C. betulus, the Hornbeam, is very similar to the beech with, if anything, a more distinguished leaf colour. In the past it was preferred to beech for hedges. Unlike beech it relishes heavy, damp soil. It will in time make a vast and dense hedge of great beauty up to at least 4.5m/15ft. Its young pliable growth makes it one of the outstanding plants for pleaching. Plant: late autumn to early spring. Planting distance: 600mm/2ft. Clip: summer.

CHAMAECYPARIS

C. lawsoniana, the Lawson Cypress, is a fast-growing conifer that prefers moist soil. The best form of hedging is *C. l.* '**Green Hedger**' which has denser foliage of a brighter green than the type. It will quickly grow into a substantial hedge (3.6m/ 12ft or more) of no great distinction. Old gardeners claim that Lawson Cypresses should be trimmed with a knife – never with shears or trimmers. Plant: winter. Planting distance: 600mm/2ft. Clip: summer-early autumn, at least twice.

 Two forms with striking upright shapes are useful for a formal garden: *C. l.* '**Allumii**' makes a slender cone of rather glaucous colour and *C. l.* '**Columnaris**' is narrowly fastigiate.

CORNUS

Cornus alba, a dogwood whose young shoots colour attractively in autumn and winter, makes an effective and unusual informal hedge up to 1.8m/6ft high. The form '**Sibirica**' has vivid red stems; '**Spaethii**' has in addition good golden variegated foliage; '**Elegantissima**' has silver variegated foliage. Plant: winter. Planting distance: 1.5m/5ft. Clip: lightly, late summer.

 C. mas, the Cornelian Cherry, has charming

small yellow flowers in February or March and attractively twisted leaves. An especially good variegated form is *C. m.* **'Aurea Elegantissima'**. It makes a decorative informal hedge of about 2.4m/8ft high. Plant: late autumn. Planting distance: 900mm/3ft. Clip: lightly, late summer.

COTONEASTER

C. simonsii is a deciduous, semi-evergreen shrub from North India with dark foliage and small white flowers in summer and handsome scarlet berries in autumn. Its young branches have an attractive brown down. It is fairly vigorous, making in time a hedge of 1.8m/6ft or more. Plant: late autumn/winter. Planting distance: 450mm/18in. Clip: late winter.

CRATAEGUS

C. monogyna, the native British Hawthorn, 'quick' or may, is a very spiny deciduous plant with aromatic white flowers in spring, an attractive fuzz of pinkish new growth in the summer and strikingly decorative haws in autumn. It makes an attractive hedge in country places, still often seen beautifully 'laid', that will grow at a fairly leisurely pace up to 3m/10ft or more. Old hedges may be successfully regenerated by cutting hard back in late summer. Plant: winter. Planting distances: 450mm/18in. Clip: late summer to early spring.

× CUPRESSOCYPARIS

× *C. leylandii*, the Leyland Cypress, is a very fast-growing conifer, introduced in the nineteenth century. It is completely hardy and resistant to winds, but its vigour means that it requires frequent clipping to keep it within bounds. It will take very hard clipping but quickly regains its – to me – unsympathetically shaggy texture. It is very successfully used at MOUNT STEWART to make a striking arcaded hedge. Plant: spring. Planting distance: 600-900mm/2-3ft. Clip: late spring/summer, at least twice.

ESCALLONIA

E. macrantha is a South American evergreen with attractive glossy foliage and small pink flowers,

but in the British Isles it is reliably hardy only in the south or by the sea. There are many cultivars available varying chiefly in colour of flower. It grows up to 3m/10ft and is not fast-growing. Plant: autumn or spring. Planting distance: 600mm/2ft. Clip: after flowering.

EUONYMUS

E. japonicus, Japanese Spindle, is an evergreen with dark, shiny green leaves which will grow slowly to a hedge of 2.4m/8ft. It is not reliably hardy except in favoured places. Variegated cultivars include **'Albomarginatus'** and the very striking gold-edged **'Ovatus Aureus'**. Plant: spring or autumn. Planting distance: 600mm/2ft. Clip: summer.

FAGUS

F. sylvatica, the Common Beech, is deciduous but in its juvenile form retains some leaves throughout the winter until new growth starts and forces off the old leaves in the spring. Clipping produces new juvenile growth and thus a clipped hedge – unlike a mature tree – will retain its leaves. Beech forms a long-living substantial hedge of an attractive shade of green in the summer turning to a handsome buff in winter. It is best as a perimeter hedge where it may be allowed to grow to a considerable height (2.4m/8ft or more). It is suitable to form internal divisions only in large gardens. Plant: late-autumn/winter. Planting distance: 450mm/18in. Clip: once, late summer.

    F. s. purpurea, the Copper or Purple Beech, comes partially true from seed but is extremely variable in leaf colour. Its mature leaf, generally a sort of muddy purple, makes a fairly gloomy hedge, but it can be an effective ingredient in some carefully planned colour scheme. Its new leaf is a dazzling fresh pink. Copper Beech is perhaps at its best as part of a mixed planting in a 'tapestry' hedge, as it is at HIDCOTE. The form most often seen is **'Riversii'**.

FORSYTHIA

F. × intermedia, the common garden forsythia (which is usually the form **'Spectabilis'**), makes an interesting informal hedge that grows quickly

to 2.4m/8ft. Its main decorative value is the profusion of yellow flowers in the spring. Plant: late autumn/early winter. Planting distance: 900mm/3ft. Clip: lightly after flowering and again in late summer.

ILEX

I. aquifolium, the native British Common Holly, with its glossy, spined evergreen foliage is a beautiful hedging plant. It makes very effective topiary, clipped into simple shapes. For berries it is essential to have male and female plants – one male to five female is the recommended proportion and some nurseries sell them in this mixture. It grows rather slowly up to 4.5m/15ft. There are many cultivars varying in leaf size and colour, but none has a more handsome appearance than the type. The cultivar *I. a.* **'J. C. van Tol'** has oval leaves with far fewer spikes. *I. a.* **'Golden Queen'** and *I. a.* **'Handsworth New Silver'** are cultivars with gold- and silver-edged leaves. The hybrid *I. × altaclerensis* has greater vigour than the common holly and has many cultivars. Plant: spring or autumn. Planting distance: 600mm/2ft. Clip: spring.

LABURNUM

The laburnum, with its spectacular racemes of yellow flowers, its pliable young wood and decorative foliage is a valuable tree for tunnels and pleaching. It should not be forgotten that all parts of this tree are poisonous. *L. anagyroides*, the Common Laburnum, is rarely used. The hybrid *L. × watereri* **'Vossii'**, freer-flowering and with especially long racemes (600mm/2ft long), is the most decorative variety. Plant: winter. Clip: tunnels and pleaching, winter; leave a quarter of the new growth and tie in.

LAURUS

L. nobilis, the Culinary Bay, makes a beautiful hedge with its reddish-brown shoots and distinguished glistening foliage. Its scent in the sun is an additional attraction. Trained as a standard and clipped into a mop-head it is very ornamental, but being a Mediterranean native it may be damaged in exceptionally severe winters. As a hedging plant it will grow fairly quickly to

3m/10ft and, even if cut down in a severe winter, will shoot again from the base. **L. n. 'Aurea'**, a gold-leaved cultivar, is in no way superior to the type. Plant: spring. Planting distance: 900mm/3ft. Clip: summer, with secateurs, avoiding cutting leaves.

LAVANDULA

The common lavender, with its aromatic grey foliage and decorative flowers makes a decorative but short-lived low (600-900mm/2-3ft) hedge. It prefers a dry, sunny site and light soil; in heavy, damp soil it is liable to die back. It should be tightly clipped, otherwise it will straggle unattractively. It may be trained as a standard and clipped into an attractive rounded head. *L. angustifolia* **'Hidcote'** is a more compact cultivar. Plant: September or spring. Planting distance: 450mm/18in. Clip: hard after flowering or in early spring.

LIGUSTRUM

There are several species of privet, deciduous and evergreen, that are useful for hedging. *L. japonicum*, the Japanese Privet, is an evergreen with dark shining foliage and, in summer, white flowers in panicles. Up to 2.4m/8ft. *L. lucidum* is similar but much more vigorous and with larger leaves. It grows up to 3.6m/12ft. *L. ovalifolium* is only semi-evergreen and may, in very cold weather, lose its leaves. It will grow in very poor soil in difficult places. *L. o.* **'Aureum'**, its golden form, is very widely seen – probably too widely. The common privet, *L. vulgare*, a European native, is not a plant of distinction. Plant: late autumn to spring. Planting distance: 200-450mm/ 8-18in. Clip: several times from spring to late autumn.

LONICERA

L. nitida, a kind of honeysuckle, is evergreen with a dense, twiggy habit. Introduced from western China in 1908, its vigour and ease of propagation rapidly established it as a popular hedging plant. It is totally hardy, takes clipping very well and has an attractive leaf colour. But it has its disadvantages. It is rather greedy and takes much goodness out of the soil. It also needs frequent

clipping; a monthly cut from May to September is not too much. This is more than most busy gardeners will feel inclined to give it. It will make a hedge 2m/6ft high or more. There is a smaller cultivar widely in cultivation called **L. n. 'Elegant'** which grows to about 1m/3ft and has a more horizontal habit than the type. Plant: late autumn/winter. Planting distance: 300mm/1ft. Clip: repeatedly, May-September.

OSMANTHUS

O. × burkwoodii has small dark green pointed leaves with an attractive sheen. It flowers in the spring – small white trumpets, with a seductive vanilla-like fragrance, borne in profusion. It will grow rather slowly to a hedge of unusual distinction – up to 2.4m/8ft high. *O. delavayi* is similar but has toothed foliage and an even greater profusion of flowers. Plant: September or spring. Planting distance: 600mm/2ft. Clip: late summer.

PHILLYREA

P. angustifolia, with its slender slightly shiny greyish leaves is a valuable and insufficiently used evergreen. It has insignificant but very fragrant flowers in spring. A species of the olive family, from the Mediterranean, it is of old use in English gardens – since at least 1597. It takes clipping very well and is valuable for simple topiary shapes and, in time, it will make a hedge of up to 1.8m/6ft. *P. latifolia* is very similar with broader slightly toothed leaves and grows much larger. Plant: autumn or spring. Planting distance: 600mm/2ft. Clip: summer.

PRUNUS

P. cerasifera, the Myrobalan or Cherry Plum, is a deciduous tree with spectacular white flowers in spring and shiny red fruit in autumn. It will make a hedge up to 2.4m/8ft high and is commonly used in mixed plantings. Plant: late autumn/ winter. Planting distance: 900mm/3ft. Clip: lightly after flowering.

P. laurocerasus, the common Cherry Laurel, is an evergreen with large glossy leaves. There are many cultivars of which one of the best is **'Otto Luyken'** with profuse flowers in racemes; much

more compact in growth than the type. It makes an open-textured hedge of at least 3m/10ft. Plant: autumn or spring. Planting distance: 900mm/3ft. Clip: with secateurs in spring or late summer.

P. lusitanica, the Portugal Laurel, is similar, but has the drawback of susceptibility to Silver Leaf disease. It clips well and makes handsome rounded topiary shapes. A very good form is the narrow-leaved *P. l.* **'Myrtifolia'**. Plant: late autumn or early spring. Planting distance: 600mm/2ft. Clip: spring or late summer, removing branches with secateurs.

P. spinosa, the Sloe or Blackthorn, is a deciduous shrub and forms a dense spiny hedge. Profuse white flowers in spring are followed in autumn by beautiful dark-purple downy fruit. For the wilder parts of a garden, perhaps as part of a mixed hedge, it has great character. It can grow to 2.4m/8ft or more. Plant: late autumn/ winter. Planting distance: 450mm/18in. Clip: lightly only, late summer.

PYRACANTHA

The pyracanthas or firethorns recommended for hedging, vary chiefly in the colour of their fruit which is designated by a cultivar name beginning with 'Orange' or 'Red' of which there are many minor variations. Tight pruning for hedges will, alas, remove the very decorative berries. They have in common attractive shining evergreen leaves and very small rather insignificant flowers. They can grow up to 3m/10ft or more. Plant: winter-early spring. Planting distance: 600mm/ 2ft. Clip: lightly from late spring to early summer, leaving a few flowers.

QUERCUS

Q. ilex, the Holm Oak, with its elegant shiny leaves with almost white undersides is one of the most distinguished of all evergreens. In more favoured sites in the south it will make a fast-growing substantial hedge of great character. Plant: spring. Planting distance: 1.2m/4ft. Clip: spring or September.

RIBES

R. grossularia, the Gooseberry, trained as a standard and with its crown gently shaped, makes a very decorative topiary specimen. Some forms have especially handsome fruit – for example **'Whinham's Industry'** has large red berries. Plant: winter. Clip: late winter and reduce new season's growth by a third in summer.

ROSMARINUS

R. officinalis, Rosemary, makes a charming informal hedge with its intensely aromatic grey leaves. It is not long-lived but clips well and has decorative blue flowers in spring. Plant: spring. Planting distance: 450mm/18in. Clip: late summer.

SANTOLINA

S. chamaecyparissus (also known as *S. incana*), Lavender Cotton, is a low-growing shrub with very dense small leaves of a grey so pale as to be almost white. It is a classic plant for edging or for filling compartments of knots and parterres. It is not long-lived and the whiteness of its leaves is most intense when young. Plant: spring. Planting distance: 300mm/1ft. Clip: spring. There is a dwarf form *S. c. nana*.

TAXUS

T. baccata, the native English Yew, is the great aristocrat of hedging and topiary plants. It lives long and, when clipped, produces dense foliage of a rich dark green – the perfect background to many plantings and a versatile structural ingredient of the garden. Perhaps its only shortcoming is that it will not tolerate waterlogged ground. There are many cultivars, some with golden foliage, but none to rival the type as a plant for hedging or topiary. *T. b.* **'Fastigiata'**, the Irish Yew, both clipped or allowed to grow naturally, is one of the most valuable of all structural plants. Plant: late autumn or spring. Planting distance: 900mm/3ft. Clip: late summer/early autumn.

TEUCRIUM

T. chamaedrys, the Wall Germander, is an evergreen with very small slightly shiny leaves and rather insignificant purple flowers. It is one of the classic ingredients of a knot garden and will grow up to 300mm/1ft. Plant: late autumn or spring. Planting distance: 150mm/6in. Clip: tightly in spring.

THUJA

T. plicata, the Western Red Cedar, in the wild grows into a tree of vast size, and it makes a vigorous but not very refined evergreen hedging plant. It prefers a moist soil where it will grow quickly to 3m/10ft and more. There are many cultivars showing different leaf colour – *T. p.*

'Atrovirens' is a good one with rich green glossy foliage. Plant: spring or autumn. Planting distance: 600mm/2ft. Clip: summer.

TILIA

The limes are the plants *par excellence* for pleaching. They have pliable young wood and foliage of decorative shape and colour. *Tilia* × *europaea*, the Common Lime, was commonly used for pleaching and for planting avenues. It has two drawbacks: it is susceptible to aphid infestation; and is prone to suckering from the base which spoils the clean lines of the trunk. The famous pleached lime walk at SISSINGHURST CASTLE, originally planted with Common Lime, was replaced in 1976 with *T. platyphyllos*. This, the Broad-leaved Lime, has much larger leaves which flutter decoratively in the breeze. Its flowers, appearing very late in July, are narcotic to bees. There is a handsome red-twigged form, *T. p.* **'Rubra'**. *T. cordata* has small, dark-green heart-shaped leaves. *T.* × *euchlora*, used for the 'walls' of pleached limes at Erddig, is, alas, susceptible to the usually fatal Slime Flux disease and is not worth risking. Plant: winter. Clip: with secateurs in winter; tying in should be done in summer during the period of maximum growth when any awkwardly growing shoots may also be removed.

STRUCTURAL FEATURES IN TRUST GARDENS

Note: This list indicates National Trust and National Trust for Scotland gardens where structural features discussed in this book may be seen: it is not a comprehensive listing of every type of feature in these gardens. *Opening Times:* Trust properties are open between April and October, but visitors are advised to telephone in advance of a visit to check times. Opening times can also be found in the *National Trust Handbook*.

Anglesey Abbey *Lode, Cambridge, Cambridgeshire (0223) 81120*
Pleaching, hedging, avenue

Antony House *Torpoint, Cornwall (0752) 812191*
Pleaching, hedging, formal pattern, avenue

Ascott *Wing, nr Leighton Buzzard, Buckinghamshire (0296) 688242*
Hedging, topiary, avenue

Ashdown House *Lambourn, Newbury, Berkshire (for opening times call NT regional office (0494) 28051)*
Formal patterns, avenue

Barrington Court *nr Ilminster, Somerset (0460) 41480*
Hedging, pleaching, pergolas, topiary, formal patterns, avenue

Batemans *Burwash, Etchingham, East Sussex (0435) 882302*
Hedging, pergola

Belton House, *Grantham, Lincolnshire (0476) 66116*
Hedging, formal patterns, avenue

Beningbrough *Shipton-by-Beningbrough, York, Yorkshire (0904) 470715*
Hedging, formal patterns, avenue

Biddulph Grange *Biddulph, Stoke-on-Trent, Staffordshire (0782) 513149*
Hedging, topiary

Blickling *Norwich, Norfolk (0263) 733084*
Hedging, pleaching, topiary, avenue

Bodnant *Tal-y-Cafn, Colwyn Bay, Gwynedd (0492) 650 460 (during office hours)*
Hedging, pergolas

Buscot Park *Faringdon, Oxfordshire (0367) 20786*
Hedging, pleaching, pergolas, avenue

Calke Abbey *Ticknall, Derbyshire (0332) 863822*
Formal pattern

Canons Ashby *Canons Ashby, Daventry, Northamptonshire (0327) 860044*
Topiary, avenue

Castle Drogo *Drewsteignton, Devon (06473) 3306*
Hedging, pleaching

Chirk Castle *Chirk, Clwyd (0691) 777701*
Topiary

Clandon Park *West Clandon, Guildford, Surrey (0483) 222482*
Hedging, formal pattern

Claremont Landscape Garden
Portsmouth Rd, Esher, Surrey (for opening times call NT regional office (0372) 53401)
Hedging, avenue

Cliveden *Taplow, Maidenhead, Berkshire (06286) 5069*
Topiary, hedging, formal patterns

The Courts *Holt, nr Trowbridge, Wiltshire (0225) 782340*
Hedging, topiary

Crathes Castle *Banchory, Kincardineshire, (033 044) 525*
Hedging, topiary

Croft Castle *nr Leominster, Hereford and Worcester (056 885) 246*
Hedging

Dunham Massey *Altrincham, Cheshire (061) 941 1025*
Hedging, avenue

Erddig *nr Wrexham, Clwyd (0978) 355314 (during office hours)*
Hedging, pleaching, formal patterns, avenue

Glendurgan Garden *Helford River, Mawnan Smith, nr Falmouth, Cornwall (for opening times call NT regional office (0208) 4281)*
Maze

Greys Court *Rotherfield Greys, Henley-on-Thames, Oxfordshire (049 17) 529*
Maze, knot garden

Ham House *Ham, Richmond, Surrey (01) 940 1950*
Hedging, pleaching, pergola, formal pattern, topiary, avenue

Hardwick Hall *Doe Lea, Chesterfield, Derbyshire (0246) 850430*
Hedging

Hatchlands *East Clandon, Guildford, Surrey*
(0483) 222787
Formal pattern

Hidcote Manor Garden *Hidcote Bartrim,*
nr Chipping Campden, Gloucestershire
(0386) 438 333
Hedging, pleaching, topiary, formal
patterns, avenue

Hinton Ampner *Bramdean, nr Arlesford,*
Hampshire (for opening times call NT regional
office (0372) 53401)
Hedging, topiary

Kedleston Hall *Derby, Derbyshire*
(0332) 842191
Pergola

Kingston Lacy *Wimborne Minster, Dorset*
(0202) 883402
Hedging, formal patterns

Knightshayes Court *Bolham, Tiverton, Devon*
(0884) 254665
Hedging, topiary, formal patterns

Lanhydrock, *Bodmin, Cornwall (0208) 3320*
Hedging, topiary, formal patterns,
avenue

Little Moreton Hall *Congleton, Cheshire*
(0260) 272018
Topiary, knot garden

Lytes Cary Manor *Charlton Mackrell,*
Somerton, Somerset (for opening times call NT
regional office (0747) 840224)
Hedging, pleaching, topiary, avenue

Montacute House *Montacute, Somerset*
(0935) 823289
Hedging, topiary, avenue

Moseley Old Hall *Moseley Old Hall Lane,*
Wolverhampton, Staffordshire (0902) 782808
Hedging, topiary, formal pattern, avenue

Mottisfont Abbey *Mottisfont, nr Romsey,*
Hampshire (0794) 40757
Hedging, pleaching, formal patterns

Mount Stewart *Newtownards, Co. Down,*
Northern Ireland (024 774) 387
Hedging, pleaching, topiary, formal
patterns, pergolas

Nymans *Handcross, nr Haywards Heath,*
Sussex (0444) 400321
Hedging, pleaching, topiary, formal
patterns

Oxburgh Hall *Oxborough, nr King's Lynn,*
Norfolk (036 621) 258
Formal patterns

Packwood *Lapworth, Solihull, Warwickshire*
(05643) 2024
Hedging, topiary, avenue

Pitmedden *Ellon, Aberdeenshire (06513) 2352*
Formal patterns

Plas-yn-Rhiw *Rhiw, Pwllheli, Gwynedd*
(075 888) 219 (during office hours)
Hedging, topiary

Polesden Lacey *nr Dorking, Surrey*
(0372) 58203
Hedging, pleaching, pergolas, topiary,
avenue

Powis Castle *Welshpool, Powys (0938) 4336*
Hedging, topiary

Shugborough *Milford, nr Stafford,*
Staffordshire (0889) 881388
Topiary

Sissinghurst Castle *Sissinghurst,*
nr Cranbrook, Kent (0580) 712850
Hedging, pleaching, topiary, avenue

Sizergh Castle *nr Kendal, Cumbria*
(053 95) 60070
Avenue

Snowshill Manor *nr Broadway,*
Gloucestershire (0386) 852410
Topiary

Standen *East Grinstead, Sussex (0342) 23029*
Hedging

Studley Royal *Fountains, Ripon, Yorkshire*
(076 586) 333
Hedging

Sudbury Hall *Sudbury, Derbyshire*
(028 378) 305
Topiary, pleaching, hedging

Tatton Park *Knutsford, Cheshire (0565) 54822*
Hedging, topiary, maze, formal patterns,
avenue

Tintinhull *Tintinhull, nr Yeovil, Somerset*
(for opening times call NT regional office
(0474) 840224)
Hedging, topiary

Waddesdon Manor *Waddesdon, nr Aylesbury,*
Buckinghamshire (0296) 651211
Hedging, topiary, formal patterns, avenue

Westbury Court *Westbury-on-Severn,*
Gloucestershire (045 276) 461
Hedging, topiary, formal patterns

West Green House *Hartley, Whitney,*
Basingstoke, Hampshire (for opening times call
NT regional office (0372) 53401)
Hedging, topiary, avenue

Wightwick Manor *Wightwick Bank,*
Wolverhampton, West Midlands (0902) 761108
Hedging, topiary

Wimpole Hall *Arrington, Royston,*
Hertfordshire (0223) 207257
Formal pattern

SELECTED READING

On the history and design of formal gardens:

Brown, Jane. *Gardens of a Golden Afternoon*, Allen Lane, 1982

Elliott, Brent. *Victorian Gardens*, Batsford, 1986

Hadfield, Miles. *A History of British Gardening*, Hutchinson, 1960

Harvey, John H. *Mediaeval Gardens*, Batsford, 1981

Page, Russell. *The Education of a Gardener*, Collins, 1962

Strong, Roy. *The Renaissance Garden in England*, Thames & Hudson, 1979

Stuart Thomas, Graham. *Gardens of the National Trust*, Weidenfeld & Nicolson, 1979

Van Der Horst, A. J. and Jacques, David. *The Gardens of William and Mary*, Christopher Helm, 1988

Inspiration and practical advice:

Bean, W. J. *Trees and Shrubs Hardy in the British Isles*, John Murray, 1970-80; Supplement, 1988

Brown, George E. *The Pruning of Trees, Shrubs and Conifers*, Faber, 1970

Clark, Ethne and Perry, Clay. *English Topiary Gardens*, Weidenfeld & Nicolson, 1988

Clevely, A. M. *Topiary; the Art of Clipped Trees and Ornamental Hedges*, Collins, 1988

Lacey, Geraldine. *Creating Topiary*, Garden Art Press, 1988

Philip, Chris. *The Plant Finder*, Headmain Ltd, 1988

SUPPLIERS

Buckingham Nurseries, 28 Tingewick Road, Buckingham MK18 4AE (Especially knowledgeable nursery specialising in trees for hedging, with efficient mail-order service.).

Andrew Crace Designs, Bourne Lane, Much Hadham, Hertfordshire SG10 6ER (Finely made trellis, arbours, etc).

Machin Designs Ltd, Ransome's Dock, Parkgate Road, London SW11 4NP (Finely made trellis, arbours, etc).

Minotaur Designs, 42 Brampton Road, St. Albans, Hertfordshire AL1 4PT (Designers of mazes).

Topiary Frames Ltd, Carriers Oast, Northiam, Rye, East Sussex TN31 6NH (Makers of ready-made frames for topiary).

I N D E X

ACKNOWLEDGEMENTS

I am extremely grateful to Penelope Hobhouse, who asked me to write this book, for the very generous interest she has taken. There is scarcely a page that has not benefited from her expert advice.

The staff of the National Trust for England and Wales, in London and in Cirencester, have been endlessly resourceful. Here, I must especially thank Mr Tony Lord, the benign Savonarola of horticultural nomenclature, who very kindly saved me from some hideous errors. The National Trust for Scotland (especially Mr Eric Robson) has also been most helpful.

The staff of the gardens that I visited were models of kindness, politely ignoring the depths of my ignorance and answering questions with exemplary patience. In particular I should like to thank: Mr Philip Cotton (Cliveden), Mr Chris Crowder (Levens Hall), Mr Michael Eales (Brickwall), Mr John Ellis (Packwood House), Mr Jimmy Hancock (Powis Castle), Mr David McLean (Crathes Castle), Miss Christine Middleton (Barrington Court), Mr Paul Nicholls (Hidcote Manor), Mr Martin Puddle (Bodnant), Mr Ian Ross (Pitmedden), Mr Chris Smith (Canons Ashby House), Mr Glyn Smith (Erddig), Mr David Stone (Mottisfont Abbey), Mr Ken Vaughan (Westbury Court) and Mr Sam Youd (Tatton Park).

I am most grateful to Mr Adrian Fisher of Minotaur Designs, who so kindly designed a maze specially for this book.

The staff of Pavilion Books, especially my Editor, Helen Sudell, have been immensely helpful. In addition, Penny David much improved my text.

My wife Caroline, herself from a deeply horticultural family, made countless improvements to the typescript and introduced me tactfully into the arcane mysteries of the relationship between parentheses and punctuation. To her I most affectionately dedicate this book.

Patrick Taylor

PICTURE ACKNOWLEDGEMENTS

All the photographs in this book were taken by the author with the exception of the following which were kindly supplied by:
The National Trust Photographic Library: pp. 14/15, 17, 18, 21, 28, 31, 36, 38, 43, 51, 55, 57, 58, 59, 60, 62, 68, 73, 80, 82, 91, 93, 94, 95; **Tony Lord**: pp. 19, 33, 35, 39, 53, 75; **Tim Rees**: p. 42

The plans were illustrated by **Lorraine Harrison.**

Adrian Fisher of Minotaur Designs kindly supplied the maze design which readers are free to copy for use in private gardens. Anyone wishing to use the design for commercial purposes should apply to Minotaur Designs for permission.